What

Mama

Taught

Me

Also by Tony Brown

*Empower the People: A Seven-Step Plan
to Overthrow the Conspiracy That Is
Stealing Your Money and Freedom*

*Black Lies, White Lies:
The Truth According to Tony Brown*

What Mama Taught Me

The Seven Core Values of Life

TONY BROWN

WM

WILLIAM MORROW
An Imprint of HarperCollins*Publishers*

Grateful acknowledgment is made to reprint from *The Collected Poems of Langston Hughes* by Langston Hughes, copyright © 1994 by the Estate of Langston Hughes. Used by permission of Alfred A. Knopf, a division of Random House, Inc.

HarperCollins books may be purchased for educational, business, or sales promotional use. For information please write: Special Markets Department, HarperCollins Publishers Inc., 10 East 53rd Street, New York, NY 10022.

FIRST EDITION

Printed on acid-free paper

Library of Congress Cataloging-in-Publication Data

Tony Brown, M.P.S.W.
What mama taught me : the seven core values of life / Tony Brown.—1st. ed.
p.   cm.
Includes bibliographical references and index.
ISBN 0-06-018869-3
1. African Americans—Social conditions.   2. Social values—United States.
3. Conduct of life.   4. Brown, Tony, M.P.S.W.   I. Title.
E185.86 .B699 2003
305.896'073—dc21   2002026580

03   04   05   06   07   WBC/QW   10   9   8   7   6   5   4   3   2   1

To all of the readers
of this book who will become
my brothers and sisters
because of my Mama

Contents

CONTENTS

Introduction

This book is inspired by Mama, an angel named Elizabeth Sanford, who saved my life, raised me, and instilled in me the core values that have guided me on my journey in this world. In fact, the book is a distillation of Mama's wisdom—wisdom it has taken me thirty years, beginning with my entry into public life in 1970, to fathom and accept. Mama was poor and without formal education—she worked as a maid and a dishwasher when she could get jobs—and I wanted to be "successful." So, I went looking for knowledge, truth, and wisdom in the place where the Establishment tells us they reside, inside the box of officially sanctioned texts, university degrees, and intellectual conformity.

I didn't deny Mama in those hallowed halls; I just didn't mention her. But as Mama used to say, revising an old saw: "He who lies down with dogs shall rise with fleas." Fortunately for me, I learned that if you live with angels, you will grow wings. I spent a lot of time in hell, too, but I did not return empty-handed. Mama's wisdom was ingrained deeply in me, and it eventually led me to a reconnection with my inner self. I spent thirty years in the desert to arrive, finally, at what Mama had taught me when I was a little boy: The key to health, wealth, and happiness is within each of us.

Even now, nearing the end of my journey, I am back with Mama—in this book. In the coming chapters, I will share with you the seven core values that she taught me and that helped me find the key to real success. My hope is that they will help you find your own key.

Mama came into my life in a mysterious way. I was born in Charleston, West Virginia, to Catherine Davis and Royal Brown. I was the fifth and last child the young couple had; the first was born when my mother was just sixteen. My father was a handsome, charming, light-skinned mulatto, a status symbol among Aframericans at that time. My mother was talented, very intelligent, and very dark, when being called black was pejorative, even among Blacks. Despite the tradition of achievement in my mother's clan, my parents' union was frowned upon by the aristocratic Browns, and their lives were made even more difficult by the rampant racism of the small Southern town. Unemployed and unable to cope, my father left for Philadelphia with another woman a couple of months before I was born. Devastated by the desertion, my vulnerable mother suffered from what I suspect was a postpartum depression so severe that she was practically incapable of caring for me. (It was always my personal opinion that my birth mother blamed me for her inability to hold my father.)

By the time I was two months old, I was near death from starvation. Miraculously, that is when Mama appeared. One day there was a knock on the door, and there was Elizabeth Sanford, with her daughter, Mabel (Mama Jr.). "We've come for the boy," Mama said. My mother pointed at the crib in the corner of the room. Nothing else was said, and for the next twelve years, until the day she died,

Mama loved me and cared for me as if I were the blood of her blood. She did not conceal from me who my parents were or keep me from seeing my biological family. Notwithstanding the fact that she game me a nickname, Sonny Boy, and addressed me by my middle name, Anthony, she made no attempt to disguise or change my name. Nor did she hide from me the facts about my biological family. The only thing she never told me was how it was that she knew that I needed to be rescued.

I am not telling this story so you will feel sorry for me or condemn my parents. That is the absolutely last thing I want, which is the main reason I have never publicly exposed my background. I do believe that parents are the rivers through which souls flow, and without Catherine Davis and Roy Brown, I would not be who I am and I would not be here to tell any story. Like all of us, they did the best with the hand that they were dealt, and I have no doubt that God has rewarded them in the fullness of His or Her loving wisdom. I do not question God's plan or my part in it; my job, the way I see it, is to learn as much as I can from every lesson that is offered and to prepare myself for the time when my angels come for me again.

The lesson I learned from Mama was the lesson of universal love: I never lacked for love. Sometimes I would not get exactly what I wanted for Christmas. Sometimes there was not quite as much food to eat or as much variety of food as I would have liked. Sometimes there was not enough money to pay the rent, and more than a few times we would hide in the darkened apartment while the landlord's man banged on the door. But there was never a shortage of hugs and kisses, never a day when I did not hear the words "I love you."

Love is the food of the soul. Life is not an event; it is a faith journey of struggles, trust, relationships, karma, learning, knowledge, wisdom, failures, and triumphs. Love is the nourishment we need to journey on and to learn the lessons necessary for spiritual growth. In a recent interview, Hugh Hefner, the founder of *Playboy,* gave a startling insight into what happens to us when love is denied. At seventy-five, Hefner boasted to *Vanity Fair* of sleeping with his harem of seven nubile women, who range in age from eighteen to twenty-eight. Yet he confessed that he is still looking for love, because his mother "never hugged or kissed" him. "And so I was always looking for that love denied me in early childhood," the *Playboy* "mack daddy" concluded.[1] The sad truth, of course, is that no amount of Viagra-pumped sex will ever take the place of a big old sloppy kiss and hug from his mama, and Hef is likely to keep looking for love, as the old song goes, "in all the wrong places."

My mama's love has been the unshakable touchstone truth of my life. No matter where I have been or what trials I have faced, the warmth and safety of her embrace have always nourished my soul. On the day she saved my life, Mama called me Sonny Boy, because, as she said, I shone like the sun. Her love allowed me to recognize the brilliance of my own spirit—to see that in God's eyes each of us is a born winner.

Self-empowerment is a weapon superior to anything that ethnic, gender, and class discrimination can throw at you. Mama's love taught me that I am a winner, and I created my success by freeing my mind and my spirit. Since 1970, I have produced and hosted more than one thousand installments of *Tony Brown's Journal,* the longest-running public-affairs series on PBS. In fact, it is now the network's longest-running series of original programs—until Fred Rogers's retirement, *Mister Rogers' Neighborhood* had been on the air four months longer than my show, according to *USA Today.*[2] The question I get from nearly everyone is "How have you made it on national television all these years?" When Blacks ask this question, there is the added desire to know how an outspoken and opinionated Black man manages to survive in a medium controlled by the White Establishment.

Unlike so many Blacks who play the race card, I ask for nothing. I don't know what White people owe us, but I do know one thing—they're not going to pay us. I have succeeded by trusting my ability to see what is possible and by staying true to the principle of self-empowerment. Your soul does not have a race or a gender, so how could your success depend on what color your skin is or on whether you are a man or a woman? As you think in your heart, so are you, to paraphrase the Bible; in other words, your ability to envision your life—reality—is what determines your success.

My message of self-empowerment has usually met with ridicule— and often full frontal professional and personal assaults—from the conventional, the imagination-impaired, and the Establishment cronies who think that I am misguided, crazy, or an uppity nigger who does not know his place. But whatever the critics may say, my out-of-the-box ideas have usually been proved right and have facilitated crucial changes in America's collective consciousness over the past three decades.

Society is rigged to encourage mediocrity through fear. The status-quo vehicle for this fear can be just about anything: your gender, class, ethnicity, educational level, religion, or country of origin. Blacks, women, and the downtrodden are prime targets for the brainwashing that teaches us to stay in our place at the bottom of the pecking order. And if you want to climb up in that order, you had better follow the rules. That is how the people in power have remained in control for thousands of years.

"Success," as it is defined by the Establishment, is learning the rules and betraying yourself and your desires. You measure your success by the most modest standards of performance—notwithstanding your enormous accumulation of money and/or degrees certifying your attendance at institutions of higher learning. The material rewards for this betrayal—money, possessions, status—are reminders of the gifts of the spirit that we have turned away from but still yearn for.

Inside this Establishment box, you are an inmate in a mental prison without walls, guarded by fear. The real you, however, is not fooled. Your spirit is crying out to recognize its true, unlimited potential and to express its need for reconnection and its natural state of happiness. Our spiritual pain is due to separation from one another, even though we are in physical proximity. Isolation from others in a four-walled prison cell or a mental prison is the most severe form of punishment that we can mete out because, as essentially spiritual beings, we crave social interaction. Without connection to the collective consciousness, we suffer spiritual death inside a living body.

This is the experience we describe as being unhappy. To dull the pain, we feed ever more greedily at the trough of materiality and "me-ism." The more we consume, the more we need, and the worse the pain becomes. In this book, I offer a foundation for both success and happiness—on your own terms.

I started my public life with a 100 percent Black orientation. I did not understand what Mama meant when she said that Blacks and Whites are foolish not to love one another. Over the years, however, I arrived at the reality that, while ethnic pride is essential to self-empowerment, ethnocentrism—the belief in ethnic superiority—is self-defeating. I learned that your mentality creates your reality and that the values you adopt determine the kind of person you become.

According to a recent article in *U.S. News & World Report,* scientists have discovered that subjective experience cannot be fully accounted for by the underlying mechanics of the brain.[3] In other words, consciousness, like space, time, or gravity, is beyond science's ability to investigate empirically or to understand.

That is another way of saying that your heart and your spirit are at the center of your experience. The only way you can duplicate anyone's success is to share the same vision of reality; the only way to win is to be yourself. Success or failure in this life is determined, literally, by what you think of yourself. The moment you accept yourself is the moment you become happy. The Establishment keeps this truth hidden in plain sight by calling it arrogance, especially if one of the non-elite happens to possess it. However, the knowledge that each of us creates his or her reality is essential to self-empowerment—to surviving as a self-respecting human being.

Mama taught me that power is an illusion if it is not the power of the spirit, that wealth is counterfeit if it is not the wealth of the heart. To me, this is the key to success and happiness. Fear and separation are inside the box; freedom and reconnection are out of the box. The choice is limitation versus unlimited possibilities. What do you want for your life? The chapters that follow will help you answer this question and will offer a blueprint for reaching spiritual balance, which is the foundation for health, wealth, and happiness.

I hope this book will act as a guide on your journey to self-fulfillment, success, and enlightenment.

1

Reality

THE VALUE OF BEING YOURSELF

Mr. Carpenter was the principal of Washington Elementary, my elementary school in Charleston, West Virginia. He was a big, tall, distinguished, good-looking man, always in three-piece suits, with his gold watch tucked neatly away in one vest pocket, anchoring his Phi Beta Kappa key, which dangled in full view. Whenever you got caught doing anything wrong, the classroom teacher would send you to Mr. Carpenter, and he would put you across his lap and give you a few licks with a barber's strap. Now, I have to admit that I was in Mr. Carpenter's office often enough that I'd gotten pretty familiar with it. And although my mind was usually on the punishment I was about to receive, I always read a quotation from

Abraham Lincoln that Mr. Carpenter had tacked on his office wall. The neatly printed card said: "Whatever you are, be a good one."

Something about those words stuck with me. I really wanted to understand them. And one day, after I had given Mama a note from Mr. Carpenter about my latest visit to his office (which was a cue to follow up with a more thorough whipping), I asked her what the saying meant. Her face went from stern and disapproving to quiet and wistful. She sat looking at me for a few moments and then said: "Sonny Boy, I think Mr. Lincoln meant that the best thing any of us can do is be good at who we are, instead of trying to be someone we are not. You are Anthony, right? If you tried to be Jackson or Rufus you wouldn't be much good at it, because that isn't who you are. But if you work at being Anthony, well, I guarantee you, you'll be a great Anthony."

I did not know it at the time, but what Mama had explained to me was the core value of reality. You see, we are taught to believe that reality is the objective world of facts, figures, and rules, and that our job is to learn how to fit into that world. But that is the Establishment version of reality—the version designed to perpetuate the status quo by producing complacent workers, consumers, and citizens. The Establishment promises health, wealth, and happiness as rewards for conformity. But it is an empty promise, because true health, wealth, and happiness come only from accepting and being yourself.

Let me tell you a story to illustrate what I mean. I spoke in San Francisco not too long ago. The audience was mostly working-class Black people. This was the first time that the majority of them had ever been to a big fancy hotel. They all looked really good in their new dresses and suits, all two thousand of them in the big ballroom—a sea of beautiful people.

I noticed this one man going from table to table. Everyone kept calling him over to their table. He was by far the most popular person in the room. I asked my host who the man was. "That's Scotty," the reverend replied. "What's he doing?" I asked. "Scotty brought the hot sauce," he said, smiling.

Somehow this crowd knew that the food "wasn't going to be right." So Scotty brought the hot sauce. And everybody had a wonderful time. They were themselves. You know how good it feels when you are just you? I wish I could have bottled up the feeling in that room to take it all over the world. These people really understood what William Shakespeare meant when he wrote:

> *This above all: to thine own self be true,*
> *And it must follow, as the night the day,*
> *Thou canst not then be false to any man.*

We are beautiful when we are ourselves. We get rid of all that baggage we are carrying around. Who is pretty? Who is ugly? Who is White? Who is Black? Who is rich? Who is poor? Who went to school, and who did not? When it is just you and me, that is when we connect with true reality.

The way to be happy is to figure out who you are and then accept yourself. We all carry our own hot sauce, whether we are aware of it or not. So the question is: What is the special ingredient you bring to the party? Once you know what it is, not only do you get to enjoy it yourself but you can also share it with others. And you know that if you bring the hot sauce, everyone is going to want you at their table. You take care of people, and they will take care of you. Everything that you do in life, if it is good, will come back to you in the form of true health, wealth, and happiness.

Reality is a powerful force. It frees your mind and your spirit from the dead weight of the "shoulds"—the pressure to conform to external concepts of your essence and your worth. You do not need to measure yourself with someone else's yardstick. All that tells you is whether you are living up to someone else's expectations. And that will never make you truly happy. What makes us happy is to be in harmony with ourselves, to live up to our inner self's, perhaps the soul's, expectations. That is being truly alive.

This may not be easy for most people to take in. We are often inclined to believe that the things we need to be happy are outside of ourselves. So when I suggest to people that the seeds of health, wealth, and happiness are within them, they often tend to be skeptical. A woman who approached me after one of my lectures not too long ago is a good example.

"Mr. Brown, I need your help. I want you to tell me how to find a good man," she said, an earnest look on her face. "All right," I said. "What sort of man are you looking for?" She had the answer all ready: "I want an honest man. A man who has a good job. Someone who is going to be a good parent." "Well, sounds like you know exactly what you want." "Yes," she said with a note of frustration. "Now, what do I do to get a man like that?" "I am going to tell you," I replied, smiling, "but you are not going to like it." She looked surprised. "Go ahead and tell me," she said. "You've got to become all those things yourself." Now she looked really impatient.

"And how is that going to help me find a man?" "In spite of what the movies would have you believe," I said, "life is not like a box of chocolates. It's much more like a bank: You can get back only what you put into it. In fact, what you attract reflects who you have become." "That's not true," she snapped back. "My boyfriend is a liar, and I'm not a liar." I responded, "Perhaps you're lying to yourself." Her expression changed. She looked at me in silence for a few moments, shook her head sadly, and said her good-byes. "Your reality is your own, and it is up to you to create it," I added.

I do not think I gave her the answer she was looking for, but I do hope that she will be able to use some of Mama's wisdom—the core value of reality—to build the kind of life she wants for herself. Amazingly often, two unhappy people come together looking to each other for happiness. The problem is that if you do not have happiness, you cannot offer it to another person. For two people to be happy, both have to bring happiness to the relationship. In other words, they have to manifest within themselves what they expect and demand from the world around them. Otherwise, it is divorce court every time or, even worse, prolonged marital misery.

Mama taught me that the moment you accept yourself is the moment you become happy—and transform your own reality and the world around you.

For me, Rosa Parks best symbolizes the transformative power of what I believe Mama meant was the core value of reality. On December 1, 1955, on a segregated bus in Montgomery, Alabama, Rosa Parks refused to surrender her seat, as the local segregation law demanded, to a White man. The popular version of the story has it that she could not, or would not, stand up because her feet hurt. But that is not the truth. Her feet might have hurt, as they probably had countless times before, but on that day Rosa Parks had an epiphany. She suddenly became conscious of the fact that Black people should never have sat in the back of the bus in the first place.

Rosa Parks's reality was that of self-respect and self-worth. And on December 1, 1955, on that bus, she manifested her reality and changed the history of her people, her country, and the world. She knew that she was a person of worth and that she should be treated as such. That is a simple statement to make today, considering the advances our society has made in race relations. But if you go back and look at the way the world was, you will see that that was hard to figure out in 1955. Most people could not get that straight. Not even Black people.

I was at Wayne State University in Detroit at the time. There were academic majors from which we were excluded, informally and formally. You could not major in geology, for example. Why? "The oil companies don't hire Black people," the advisers said. "So why would you invest four years in geology and not be able to get a job?" We were also discouraged from majoring in psychology or television and radio. Nobody would hire an Aframerican for jobs in those fields. It was just accepted as fact that you could not do certain things that society did not want you to do. In Detroit, for instance, Blacks were practically barred from working at banks.

After the Rosa Parks Montgomery Epiphany, we saw the falseness of those barriers. Suddenly, we said to ourselves, "Why are we taking this? I put my money in the bank, but I can't work at the bank? I pay taxes to pave the streets on the east side of this city, but I can't live on the east side of this city? No, there's something wrong with that picture. That dog won't hunt." And the reality of this country was changed forever.

Rosa Parks gave external form to her internal reality, to the image she had of herself. And on that historic day, she became the heart of the Civil Rights movement and a symbol to fair-minded people everywhere. When Rosa Parks refused to give up her seat to a White man on that bus in Montgomery, Alabama, Black people all over America stood up with a new sense of consciousness—a consciousness of self-empowerment.

The Realities of My Childhood

It was not until I began to think about this book that I realized to what degree Mama has shaped my life—and to what extent she remains a mystery for me even to this day.

I still do not know how Mama knew that I needed to be rescued as a baby. She told me the story at one point, but it did not really explain how she knew. She said that she had heard there was a boy whose mother was struggling, and so she went to look. That may be true, but somehow I did not buy it. There always seemed to be something a little deeper there. Even our tremendous physical resemblance was perplexing, and a little eerie. We had the same complexion, same features, everything. You never would have known she was not my biological mother unless I told you.

Mama came to Charleston from a little town called Pax, West Virginia. I spent one summer there with her aunt. It was like any other small rural town, nothing distinguished about it. Just a Norman Rockwell town, with Black people in it, eking out a living. Lights went out at six or seven o'clock. Whenever it got dark was when everyone went to bed. They woke up when the sun came up, and every day was just like the day before, except for Sunday, when everyone went to church. That was it.

I liked it in Pax. I had big fun. I played with the animals and rode horses and did all the fun summer stuff. But that is as much of a glimpse into Mama's history as I ever got. Today, I do not even have a picture of her. There was one picture that she gave me, but when she died, her Pax aunt came to the funeral and took it from me. I was only twelve, and I was devastated at having to give up the only picture of Mama I had.

I am still sad about it, and that incident, like all the pieces of the story, just adds to the mystique of Mama. What I do know is that Mama was a very intelligent and intuitive woman. She was not formally educated, but she had a lot of faith and had a vision of herself that was fairly complete in some ways. She was very secure with her reality.

Mama must have been about forty years old when she got me. By that point, I think she had gotten a lot of experience from hitting some bumpy roads, a Black woman alone in the world. Her daughter, Mabel, was already grown when Mama took me in. Although they were mother and daughter, they were also kind of sisterly. So I think Mabel may have been born when Mama was very young. There was never mention of a man. It was pretty much two women struggling out in the world.

Mama was a very good-looking woman, and she had the men in her age-group pursuing her. But I never saw her really get involved. I sensed that she had gone through a sea change and decided: "That's over. I finished that part, that boy-girl business. And there are other things I want to do with my life. I want to serve God." She was devoutly religious, but not preachy.

Mama taught me the value of reality over and over, in words and by example. "Other people can only tell you who they want you to be," Mama would say to me. "You've got to find out for yourself who you are." My teachers told me to become a lawyer because of my speaking skills. Following their well-meaning advice, I tried going down that path but found little satisfaction.

I laugh now when I think about my youthful arrogance in dismissing Mama as not knowing anything about success. My idea was that being successful meant getting out of Charleston, going to college, making money—all the things Mama had not done.

What I did not realize until much later in life was that I knew how to succeed because Mama had taught me to know and accept myself—to first see myself as a success.

I have to admit that I am ambitious. I have wanted to be successful ever since I came out of my mother's womb. I never ever wanted somebody else to tell me what to do. And I figured out really early that if I had enough money, I would not have to take orders from anybody else. So, for as long as I can remember, I always wanted to get some money and become independent. When I was six years old, I had saved up enough money somehow to buy two chickens. Well, chickens do what they do. They started laying eggs and hatching, and within weeks I had about sixty chickens. We had no place to keep so many chickens. They were overrunning the yard and the house. Mama said, "Sonny Boy, you've got to do something with these chickens. You've got to sell them."

So I went to the local grocery store and negotiated with the owner, and he agreed to buy the chickens. He gave me a pretty fair price; it must have been about five dollars. I went home and paraded those chickens down to the store. There I was, six years old, marching through the neighborhood like a Pied Piper with these sixty chickens. I will never forget how I felt when the grocery store owner gave me the five dollars. I was about to burst with pride and self-satisfaction. It was like I was a Wall Street corporate raider who had just bought Microsoft. I triumphed. And from that day on, I have never been without a business, in fact, more than one business.

I suppose that was Mama's way of teaching me about success—about creating my own reality. She saw the ambition in me, the entrepreneurial bend, and she guided me gently toward acting on those innate qualities. Nowadays, especially in the Aframerican community, it is very fashionable to say, "Let's motivate the young people." So we lecture them to death. "You're Black, and you're proud," we tell them. "Feel good about what you are. Benjamin Banneker did this, Sojourner Truth did that. You can do it too."

Although the thought is admirable, I believe a more effective way to motivate a child is by helping that child succeed at doing something he or she loves. Encourage the child to develop a skill: Learn to play the piano. Learn to run fast. Learn to draw. Learn to dance and sing. Learn to use a computer. The reward is the sense of mastery and confidence you get when you do something well, when you accomplish a goal. That was the lesson Mama gave me about creating a success reality: You want to feel confident? You want to be successful? Sell some chickens.

That was how Mama taught me everything. I remember learning to read with her when I was a little boy. We had this game. We would walk down Washington Street, the main street in Charleston. That is where the five-and-dime store was, where the fancy men's store and all the other nice stores were. We would walk down the street, with her holding my hand, and Mama would encourage me to read the names written on the stores. She would say, "What is that one?" And I would say, "That's Kaufman Brothers." And on we went like that, the whole length of the street. I always looked forward to going down Washington Street with her, because I felt so good showing Mama how well I could read.

That was Mama's way of parenting, like mentoring. She would see the talents in me and encourage them. When I was in the fourth grade, for instance, I wanted a drum so I could be in the band. There was only one Black band in town, the Garnet High School band. In order to get into the band, you had to buy an instrument and a uniform. In addition, if you were not in high school or you were a beginner, you had to have expensive music lessons from Dr. Maude Wanzer Lane, the high school music teacher and the band's director. She was an extremely brilliant woman, with a Ph.D. from the Sorbonne in Paris.

In any case, joining the band was an expensive proposition, especially for Mama. I remember that the uniform alone cost $35. That would probably be about $350 today. But Mama somehow scraped the money together and bought me a drum, a uniform, and music lessons. I do not know how she did it, but she did. So, in the fourth grade, I became a member of the famous Garnet High School band.

Mama would see things in me and, making enormous sacrifices, would encourage my growth, my expression of my reality. As long as it was productive, she encouraged it. I remember getting the notion one day to become a bodybuilder like Charles Atlas. And that Mama did not go for. She said, "Boy, that's just vanity. You don't need all those dumbbells. You want to exercise, go run." I ended up running track, and I was fairly good at distances. Again, Mama had paved the road to build my confidence.

There was, of course, another dimension to how Mama was raising me. You have to remember that we are talking about a time when racism and segregation were the norms in this country. So, Mama taught me that the only way up from being poor and around racism is through education, that success is the best form of revenge (although Mama would never have put it that way). She taught me to accept reality rather than get bogged down in how things should be. "Life is like a footrace," Mama told me once when I was complaining about how much homework I had to do. "You have to run a hundred yards with a fifty-pound sack on your back and beat the White boy to the end of the line. And he won't have a fifty-pound sack on his back. Now, that's not fair, but until things change, that's the way the race is. If you want to win, you have to be stronger and smarter."

Here, I want to explain the environment in our Charleston, West Virginia. The race problem in this country began during a forty-year period after the first twenty Africans arrived in Jamestown, Virginia, in 1619, as indentured servants. The importation of Black slaves began in 1629 into Connecticut, and in 1641 into Massachusetts, which became the first colony to legalize slavery. Racism and segregation were deliberate inventions of men who developed a system to make money by separating Blacks and Whites.

My childhood world was mainly the world of Black people that existed in America since the first twenty Africans arrived as immigrants. Like everything else in the Charleston, West Virginia, of my youth, the school system reflected this racially segregated America. My elementary school was named after Booker T. Washington—the famous Aframerican educator and the first White-media-selected leader of Black America at the turn of the twentieth century—not George Washington, the White man who was the nation's first president, because our school system was racially divided.

West Virginia is a border state that seceded from the state of Virginia in 1863 mainly because the White people in the western part of Virginia did not want slavery. As a result, the culture in West Virginia was quite different from that in neighboring Virginia and the Deep South. Even though there was segregation, it was not strident and it was without the racial violence of a Mississippi or an Alabama of that era. Instead, there was a glimmer of hope for Black people, especially in the public education system, which was, in my case, uniquely excellent.

Blacks were not legally required to sit in the back of the bus. The library was never segregated. We could try on clothes in stores. There was an informal separation of the "races," but no legal housing segregation. There were always interracial unions and plentiful examples of exogamy in a highly miscegenated Black population. Black children and White children could play together, and my best friend until my teen years was a White neighbor.

Do not get me wrong, it was segregated and racist enough for you to hear the word *nigger* fly from the mouths of Whites, to become depressed because you did not have the same opportunities or future as a White person, to know that, with the exception of education, you were deliberately being underdeveloped and limited in many ways, to know you were not treated fairly, to know you were deprived of your basic rights as a human being, and always to wonder why any humane society would systematically treat people this way.

You always hurt, and you had to manage the rage in order to avoid creating even bigger problems—especially if you were a Black male, the main object of racist fear. West Virginia society may have treated Blacks better than Mississippi society did, but racism was a fact of life—and it was demeaning and evil.

We could not go into White restaurants. We could not go to the White movie houses. That hurt me more than anything, because I loved movies. We had our own movie house, owned by a man named Captain Ferguson, whose daughters, Barbara and Betty, and niece, Carol Stoval, were legendary beauties. So we could go to the Ferguson Theater, but we could not go to the major theaters and see the first-run films.

Segregation in Charleston was unique. There was not the brutal oppression of the South. We were not fighting White people. They were not fighting us. We just had a world, and they had a world. We would meet downtown, getting on the buses, getting off the buses, going into stores, and so on. Some Blacks and Whites met clandestinely after dark for other purposes. But, basically, there were few White people in my world, mainly those I would see on the street.

The White people in Charleston may have been racist, but they were not vicious. They did not want to live with us, and they made no bones about that. If they could have had their druthers, we probably would not have been around. But they were not bent on destroying us. They were not going to give us jobs, but they were not going to stop us from being well prepared, either. They did not set up a school system to keep us ignorant. The White schools and Black schools were as close to being separate and equal as I have ever seen.

West Virginia is a peculiar state in this way. It is very poor state, but the public school system in West Virginia, even today, is way up in the national ratings. It has always been committed to the fundamentals: You learn to read. You learn to write. You learn to compute and reason. Education is very important. So the schools were not separate but unequal. We did not have the same equipment as the White school, but we had very good equipment. And, most important, we had the very best teachers. It was a perverse benefit of segregation. When so-called integration, or desegregation, came, our Black teachers became the stars in the formerly White school system.

The proof of the pudding, as they say, is in the eating. We graduated about fifty to seventy students a year from Garnet High School, the Black high school in Charleston. My guess is that around 90 percent of the students who graduated from our school went to college. It was not unusual for a Garnet graduate to attend the most prestigious schools in the United States, such as Harvard, Yale, and the University of California. However, for the most part, we graduated from one of the historically Black colleges, mostly from nearby West Virginia State College.

Nevertheless, ambitious Blacks who wanted to improve upon or market this excellent education had to head north or west. This benign form of racism seemed to be designed to educate Blacks so they could leave Charleston and settle elsewhere if they wanted occupational opportunities. Therefore, for generations, future medical doctors and research scientists, such as Jack Norman and Bernard Dyer, went to Howard and Harvard and then settled in other communities to share the human capital and the lifesaving skills that Charleston did not want from its brilliant Black children.

They are part of a literal army of Black professionals who were forced to emigrate and enrich other communities with their skills, like Lewis Smoot, my classmate, did after graduating from Michigan State University with his multimillion-dollar construction business based in Columbus, Ohio. As a result of the racial exclusion, many of us left the economy and the culture of West Virginia poorer, only to demonstrate sadly, once again, that there are no winners in a racist society.

I had no idea how well-respected Garnet was academically until I got to Wayne State University. In the beginning of the first term, all freshmen anticipated taking an entrance exam. A group of us were waiting in a big auditorium. Being in a White environment for the first time in my life nourished the fear of the racial unknown. A proctor came in and called my name. He said, "You're Brown?" I said, "Yes, sir." He checked his papers and said, "Well, you don't have to take the exam, you're exempted." "Why?" I asked the White man, all nervous inside. "I knew it," I said to myself, confirming my fears of being rejected because I was Black. "You're not going to let me in?" "Oh, no"—he smiled—"we're going to admit you." "Well, why don't I have to take the test, then?" I insisted, thinking that there must be some catch. He smiled again and said, "Well, because of the quality of your high school."

In hindsight, I recognize that we were prepared to go to the best schools in the United States because the teachers had a purpose and a system to prepare us for the best schools. And they were the crème de la crème, these teachers were. Many had Ph.D. degrees in their disciplines.

Mrs. Ruth Norman, who is one of my heroes, was our high school English teacher. She was a dominant force in our school and the community, because she was an extremely capable and talented person. Every day when the bell would ring in her class, Mrs. Norman would say: "So much to learn, and so little time to learn it in." That was our unofficial motto. We were conditioned to repeat these words when the bell rang. And all the teachers, our parents, and the whole community reinforced these core values.

The school, the teachers, the institutions, the families, they all taught us that education was a precious opportunity. We were taught to study not for tests but for life. The worst punishment that any of us young people could have gotten was being put out of school. There was no greater disgrace. There was no greater isolation than being expelled from school. Because, when I went to school, even the worst student wanted to go to college. Even the worst student was a gentleman or a lady. This does not just happen. This was the product of the investment our community made in its children. It was the product of the wealth—the intellectual, spiritual, and social wealth—of the Aframerican community in my hometown.

We might have lived in a segregated world, but we knew that our whole community was making sure that we got an equal opportunity to learn. This was probably the biggest influence in shaping the reality of my childhood. I came out of a Black culture that was equal to the White culture.

There were two big Black churches in Charleston: the First Baptist Church and the Memorial Methodist Church. I was a Methodist. Dr. Mordecai Johnson was the minister of the First Baptist Church. He was recruited from First Baptist to become the most famous president that Howard University (the capstone of Black higher education, where I would, years later, become the founding dean of the School of Communications) has ever had. He was succeeded at the church by the Reverend Moses Newsome, who was a philosophy professor at West Virginia State College. So often the Sunday school teacher was a college professor.

Our community had a lot of scholarly people. It had the nurturing environment of a college town. It was a culturally rich place. We did not consider it out of the ordinary that our school had a speech choir and a debating society. It was not noteworthy for us that we had a glee club, a cheerleading squad, and a band. We had basketball, football, and drama. In a Black school, we had a forensic society. We had a High-Y Club, where we learned to be civic leaders. Our band traveled and performed all over the country.

We had town forums where the whole community came to the high school to hear and see famous Black people like the scholarly Dr. Benjamin Mays, president of Morehouse College, and Paul

Robeson, the quintessential Renaissance man (Phi Beta Kappa scholar, all-American athlete, singer, movie actor, and so on). The night Paul Robeson was there, all these White people were in the audience. I had never seen a White person in one of these meetings, so I was really surprised. It turns out that they were all FBI agents, there watching the internationally renowned Mr. Robeson, who was, in their minds, a subversive. We went to enjoy his performance and the resonant power of his soulful voice.

This was the intellectual environment in which I grew up. And I flourished in it. I remember when I was in elementary school, there was a teacher, Dr. Della Brown, who lived near me. I would hide out in the morning so I could accidentally bump into her as she walked to school and walk with her. On the mornings when I did not do that, I would get to the school an hour early, at seven o'clock. I would stand outside until the janitor saw me and let me in. And I would sit and talk to him as he stoked the furnace, because I could not wait to go to class. I do not remember anything I did that was more exciting than being in a classroom where I was learning.

I was an eager student, and I had a talent for speaking. So I got a lot of encouragement from my teachers. In the first grade the stage play was always *Little Boy Blue.* I was selected to be Little Boy Blue. From then on, I was in every school production there was.

When I went from elementary school to junior high school, the teachers had anticipated my arrival. They had an entire program of things they wanted me to do on the stage—being the emcee at events, speaking at assemblies, giving the opening address at a town meeting. And when I got to high school, Mr. William Barnes, the renowned drama coach, was waiting to develop my budding skills. He had an entire year of plays and roles laid out around me. George in *Our Town* and Cassius in *Julius Caesar* are two examples. By the twelfth grade, I was directing as well.

The teachers passed me along in an informal thespian farm system, not unlike one for a promising athlete. Performing arts at Garnet were almost on a par with athletics, and in my case the teachers had recognized the germ of something that could be developed. The more they told me I was good, the better I became, because then I was not afraid to take a chance. The teachers reinforced the basic skills and innate talents that Mama had identified and fostered. And the more I succeeded, the more I was willing to try things. The more confident I became, the less fear I had of failure. That was the genesis of my belief that if you are afraid to fail, you are afraid to succeed.

When I graduated from Boyd Junior High School, I was elected the most all-around boy in my class. And that is basically what I was. I ran track. I played football until the other guys got too big. I was good in intellectual pursuits. I won a statewide history contest. I was good in drama. In high school, I was president of the High-Y Club. I was the director of the speech club. I was president of the Forensic Society. I was president of the glee club. I was president of my class from the seventh grade through the twelfth grade. I was the drama guy all through high school and the one teachers relied on to memorize long parts. And, always, I was a good public speaker.

I did make the mistake of trying to mimic Billy Eckstine and sing "Blue Moon" in a high school talent contest. I was laughed off the stage—by my best friends. To succeed as a singer in the Black community, good is not enough. During my day, you had to be a Chuck Jackson, Dinah Washington, or Aretha Franklin, because in every Black community there was an Apollo Theater "hook" ready to drag a nonsinging Tony Brown off the stage. (A few years later, I failed miserably the test to qualify for training as an Air Force pilot.)

All of us have skills that other people do not have. None of us has a monopoly on talent, but our talent must be recognized and encouraged, or it will not develop. All of us were encouraged to pursue areas where we had demonstrated potential. Mama and my teachers were there for me, thank God. Had they not seen my talents and encouraged me, I would not have gotten the confidence to develop my skills, to formulate a vision of myself as a success, and to manifest my reality.

You Are Who You Believe Yourself to Be

As good a place as Charleston was to grow up, it was no place for an ambitious young Black man to live. Mama died when I was twelve, and my sister Billie, who was six years older than I, took over as my surrogate mother. By the time I finished high school, I knew that I had to seek my fortune out in the world. I lived to leave Charleston, West Virginia. I could not wait to get out of town. I graduated from high school on Friday night, borrowed sixteen dollars from my brother Nathan, and was on a bus to Detroit on Sunday morning.

I arrived in Detroit on a hot, muggy Sunday night on my first foray out into the world, the beginning of my quest for fame and fortune, with about three dollars left in my pocket. Natalie, my father's sister, lived in the city, so I went to live with her. During her visit home for a funeral, she had given me the idea of going to Wayne State University. Natalie had little money. She and her family lived in the real slums. I was poor in Charleston, and at one time I lived in a slum, but we did not have slums like the ones I saw in Detroit. Being poor in Charleston was very different; it was closer to being middle class, when compared with Detroit. I was in for a real shock.

My aunt had two sons and a daughter, a few years younger than I: William, Charles, and Frances, who was named after one of our other aunts, a beautiful showgirl at the famous Cotton Club in Harlem, where only Whites could attend as customers. Natalie and her family were lovely people, and they were so happy to see me. To celebrate my arrival, my aunt invited a few people over. Her boyfriend was there, along with some other Black men from the neighborhood.

We were sitting in the living room, and they were all taking turns telling stories about how there were no jobs in Detroit. It was a tale of defeat. They felt that fate had them by the throat. Nobody could find a job. "You go out to the factories; they're not hiring at Ford, not hiring at GM." It was like a victims' chorus, and all the words seemed as if they had been rehearsed. They believed there were no jobs in Detroit, and they could not find jobs. That was their reality. They did not sound like Mama.

I had a special interest in what they were saying, since I had to figure out not only how to get into college but also how to pay for it. I was sitting there, seventeen years of age, literally just off the bus, and I reflexively responded to the situation. "Excuse me," I began. I think I might have even raised my hand for permission, out of habit. "What is the richest White restaurant in Detroit?" "Oh, that's Al Green's," someone answered reverently. I asked, "How do I get there?" "Well, you walk down to the end of this street, to Woodward, and you get on the streetcar. You go to the end of the line and you get a transfer. That costs another nickel. You go to the end of the line on the transfer, and you're in Grosse Pointe." "What's Grosse Pointe?" I wondered. "Oh, that's where the richest White people live." Someone else added enthusiastically, "When you get off the streetcar, walk one block, and you'll see Al Green's." I thanked them for the information, now knowing what the first step of my quest would be.

The first thing the next morning, I got up, took the streetcar to Grosse Pointe, and found Al Green's. I was a Black boy from the South, so I knew I had to go to the back door. In many ways, things in the North were no different for Blacks than they were in the South. So, I went around back to the kitchen. I knocked on the door, and when a man answered, said, "Do you need a bus——" Before I could say "boy," he virtually grabbed me by the collar and pulled me into the restaurant. "Do we need a busboy? Thank God." And I was hired as a busboy immediately. My quest had begun.

All through high school, I had helped my debonair oldest brother, Paul, who was a waiter at the country club in Charleston. I was familiar with the aristocratic WASP culture, because Paul schooled me in its nuances. I knew how rich Anglo-Saxons behaved socially and culturally. So I knew how to fit in as an employee. Two weeks after I got hired, I was a waiter. Two weeks after that, I was the assistant captain, standing in one of the most famous, richest restaurants in Detroit in a little tuxedo.

My job as the assistant captain was to seat people in the most elegant performance I could muster and to help the captain supervise the waiters. I was really a glorified mascot, but that is what they wanted, and I was what rich White people liked in their servants, compliant and subservient, with good manners. I especially liked seating my favorite regulars, the ex-showgirl Greg Sherwood and her filthy-rich, scion husband from the Buhl clan of moneyed automakers. Fortunately, I was their favorite, too.

When I got promoted, the Black captain told me how the system worked: "When people come in, you ask for their reservations and take them to their table. Just remember, we cannot seat any Negroes or Jews." That was the first time I realized that Blacks were not the only people who did not get equal treatment. All I knew back home in Charleston was Black and White. I did not know there also was a rift between White people based on religion. I realized that Al Green, who owned the restaurant, was a Jew, and the captain noted that it was ironic that Green, theoretically, could not eat in his own restaurant.

In spite of my budding social consciousness as an immigrant from the South, I did very well for myself. Over a period of three months, I had earned about five thousand dollars, which was possible only because of the gratitude of Mr. Buhl on behalf of his beautiful Greg, who affectionately called me Brownie and tipped me lavishly. That was all the money in the world at that time. And that is how I got through the first year and a half of college, before I was drafted into the Army.

Back then, your draft board always remained in your hometown, no matter where you moved. Although I was in college in Detroit, my White "friends and neighbors" (that is what the local draft board called itself) back in Charleston thought that it would be better if a Black college student up North took his chances on getting killed, rather than their sons. It turned out to be the greatest thing that ever happened to me. I was messing around in college, caught up in the whole social scene, with too much freedom, too many temptations, and too little maturity. My priorities were in the wrong place. I was not a serious student, despite the fact that I believed I was studious. I was, overall, very confused, and had I stayed on this course, I would have ruined my one and only chance to succeed in college.

The Army gave me the structure and time to get myself straightened out. And here again, my entrepreneurial skills came in handy. We recruits were issued fifty dollars when we went in, to buy soap and toothpaste and such. I bought just the basic necessities, and kept around forty out of the fifty dollars. Everyone else spent their fifty dollars on the first day. They were broke, and there was another four weeks to go before we got any more money. So I began to lend money at interest.

I would also sell candy when we were out training in the field. I would buy a box of candy for maybe a dollar, sell it, and make five or eight or ten dollars. I was doing so well, I hired this real big guy to guard me, so I would not get beaten up and robbed. After two years in the Army, I had saved several thousand dollars.

The Army was the first and most egalitarian system I had ever been a part of; as recruits, after taking an oath to die for America, we were bluntly told by a White southerner that equality was the military's formal policy. With some exceptions, you rose to the place where you belonged. Unlike American society, the military was at least trying. I was ultimately stationed in a newly desegregated unit, the 232nd Field Artillery Battalion, a former racially segregated Alabama National Guard unit that had been activated and sent to Neu Ulm, Germany, the birthplace of Albert Einstein. I became the first Black to work in the personnel department, the highest-placed Aframerican in the battalion, after I had gone to a leadership school in the United States for advanced training and received an early promotion for graduating in the top five. I graduated number two in my class of thirty (seventy had begun the program).

Typical of the Army, I had been given special training in various techniques of killing and combat leadership, then assigned to an administrative job. I was soon promoted to battalion clerk of the 232nd, which meant, among other things, that I unofficially ran the court-martial proceedings as the assistant to the battalion sergeant major. I was in charge of recording and supervising the records of the officers of the entire battalion, an unheard of responsibility for an eighteen-year-old Aframerican in that former Dixie outfit. There were no Black commissioned officers, and other than a sergeant or two, there were no Blacks in charge of anything in the 232nd. I like to think that the way I used my sensitive position saved many an innocent Black soldier (and a goodly number of Whites) from long stints in jail.

The Army I was in was a draft Army, so it was a demographic replica of the nation's population. The Army today is not representative of the U.S. population; it is only representative of the non-elitist classes. But the Army I was in, Harvard was there, Yale was there, hillbilly was there, poor Black from Mississippi was there. Everyone in our society was "in the house," and in that environment, I succeeded. I had to use my cunning at times. I had to duck and dive. But despite the fact that racism was ever present, I learned that I could go up against the best that this country had. I learned that I could earn money. I learned that I could succeed in a competitive system. I made corporal a year ahead of schedule—and White people were promoting me. I discovered what I was made of, and I learned to have more and more confidence in myself.

All along, Mama's core value of reality guided me. I had a vision of myself as a success, and I succeeded. By success, I do not mean that I always came in first. Sometimes it meant second or fifth place, and many times I succeeded by winning only the inner battle for a personal best. When I returned to Wayne State, I renounced my old habits, because I knew for the first time how valuable college could be in my attempt to better my condition. I soon discovered that I loved psychology. I could not major in psychology because it was not practical for me to finish a doctoral program, but I could get my first degree in sociology, which I also loved, with a minor in psychology. I did that, then received a scholarship for a two-year program for a master's degree in psychiatric social work. I worked as a psychiatric social worker for three years. I loved it, and I was good at it. But I discovered that it was not where I wanted to be every day for the rest of my life.

I got involved in drama again as a hobby. I used to write and produce plays locally, because Blacks in Detroit did not have a theatrical outlet. I would put up my paycheck, rent a hall, pay the royalties on a play, advertise and promote it ("Tony Brown presents . . ."), and hope I could sell enough tickets to get the money back. Most times, I never did get the money back, but I was putting on plays and learning, and that made me happy. I got good at putting on plays, because that was what I liked to do.

In many of the shows, I would play a leading role and direct as well. Those days included Walter Mason, who in today's climate would have been a major movie star (he is the creative director for stage shows at the Hilton in Las Vegas). Also there at the time was my fellow thespian Elliott Hall, who today is a former powerful vice president of dealer development and minority operations at Ford Motor Company. If Blacks then had had today's opportunities in movies and entertainment television, Elliott and I would have been shoo-ins for the Eddie Murphy or Chris Rock genre—without the dirty mouths. However, I am sure that Elliott is much more pleased with things the way they turned out; I know that I am.

One day I decided that, in order to promote my plays, I would write a little drama column for the *Detroit Courier,* the local edition of the last national Black newspaper chain, the famous *Pittsburgh Courier.* When I talked to the editor, I was pretty full of myself, so I laid it on: "I'm real smart; I've got a master's degree and all that. I can write circles around anybody. Tell you what, I'll do you a favor and write a column." I was arrogant enough to believe that college had made me smart—and, for some strange reason, a journalist.

The editor, the crusty (until you got to know him) Chester Higgins, had his own wry brand of con, too: "I'll tell you what. I don't have any money to pay you, and you don't know how to write, so you really have nothing to sell. But if you want to learn to write, you've come to the right place. I'm a professional writer. I can teach you if you want to work for the experience."

When I wrote my very first article for the *Detroit Courier,* I knew that I had found what I wanted to do for the rest of my life. So, over the next five years, I never received a paycheck from the paper, but Chester Higgins taught me how to be a journalist.

I started out with a column on theater. Then I moved up to news articles for the city section, then feature stories for the national edition. I would go home on a typical Friday night around eight o'clock. I would write until two or three in the morning. Then I would rush over to a club and interview someone like Duke Ellington or Count Basie for a feature article. Then I would get back home at four or five in the morning, write the story from five till eight or ten, and run down to the paper at eleven o'clock to turn the story in before my deadline. Sammy Davis, Jr. was my favorite subject, and we developed a love-hate relationship that spilled over into my television days.

I was so happy with what I was doing, I was not even tired. I was working for myself. I could have done that twenty-three hours a day for the next 5 million years. I had never been so excited about anything in my life, because I had finally found my niche. I discovered that I was a journalist and set out to manifest that reality.

I developed the concept of advocacy journalism, which was objective but not apologetic. The White media were defending the status quo of racism. We did not shy away from calling a racist a racist. We did not use objectivity as an excuse not to tell the truth. And we were not afraid to explore new ideas and ways of looking at things, no matter how far-out they might have seemed.

That was the foundation on which *Tony Brown's Journal* was built, subjective objectivity based on the principle of fairness. For over thirty years now we have explored the world that we share, challenged the status quo, and changed the face of American television. What I have learned on that journey is that the only way to be truly successful is to be happy with who you are and what you do. Mama's lesson about the value of reality has stayed with me, and I found a way to create a reality of true success.

We all have a built-in guidance system that is designed to help us create our reality—our inner voice. Your inner voice may be soft, it may be really hard to hear, but it is there. You have to take time to listen. Practice listening. That voice will lead you to who you are and what you are. And once you discover that, you can accept yourself and be happy. The reality of health, wealth, and happiness is yours to create. Just remember what Mr. Lincoln said: "Whatever you are, be a good one."

When I look back, what strikes me is that the people who molded my life were all happy being themselves. In addition to Mama and my older sister Billie, I have three heroes: Mrs. Ruth S. Norman, Mr. William Barnes, and Dr. H. Naylor Fitzhugh.

Mrs. Norman, a Howard University graduate and a prominent member of the national Alpha Kappa Alpha sorority, was my high school grammar teacher. There will never be a finer woman. She was a lady in the truest sense of the word. She was articulate. She was literate. She was fair. She quoted all of these famous people and told you what it meant in terms of your life. Her favorite quotation was from Shakespeare, from *Hamlet:*

> *This above all: to thine own self be true,*
> *And it must follow, as the night the day,*
> *Thou canst not then be false to any man.*

I produced a TV show about Mrs. Norman, and we had one of the heaviest waves of mail ever. Everyone had the same response: "That is my teacher." They all saw their teacher in Mrs. Norman, because of her values.

Mr. William Barnes was my high school literature teacher. He was a very handsome, distinguished man, who dressed like a Yalie. He also headed the drama department and selected me for all those plays in which I appeared. He went to a Black men's college named Lincoln in Pennsylvania. He was also quick to remind us: "I'm a Lincoln man." That meant that he stood for something—for good values.

He was brilliant, too. He spoke Middle English—Chaucer's English—as eloquently as you and I speak standard English. He had truly mastered his subject. I really looked up to Mr. Barnes and wanted to be like him. I even wanted to dress like him. As a matter of fact, the first pair of glasses I got were glasses like Mr. Barnes used to have.

Finally, Dr. H. Naylor Fitzhugh was my mentor, who guided me through my professional life for many years. After beginning college at sixteen and graduating from Howard, he became the second Black to graduate from Harvard with an M.B.A., around 1931. When he got his degree, the only job that was offered to him was that of checkout clerk in an A & P supermarket. That was what business meant for Blacks with M.B.A.s from Harvard at that time.

Instead, Dr. Fitzhugh took a job at Howard University, teaching business classes, and little by little he defined and organized what we know today as the School of Business and Administration at Howard University. Later he became a vice president, the second Black, at the Pepsi-Cola Company, which is when I met him. He mentored many of the very well-known Black business pioneers, like Earl Graves, the publisher of *Black Enterprise* magazine.

I first met Dr. Fitzhugh when I lived in Detroit, before I moved to New York to work on *Tony Brown's Journal.* He encouraged me enormously. He told me once: "Everybody is not an entrepreneur. You are. You would risk the rent on what you believe in. That's how you know you are an entrepreneur."

I have been really blessed in my life. I have had incredible people to help me along the way. How did I get to where I am? I got to where I am because of people who loved me and took the time out to help me and to manifest my reality. And all of them had one quality in common: They had mastered the core value of reality. They knew who they were, and they were happy. Mama was happy. Mrs. Norman was happy. Mr. Barnes was happy. Dr. Fitzhugh was happy. None of them was rich, but they were all extremely wealthy people. They possessed true wealth—measured in self-worth rather than net worth.

At this point, you might be saying, "Fine, but how do I go about creating my own reality?" The answer is deceptively simple: Be yourself, no matter what anybody else tells you you should be. Bill Russell is an excellent example of the power of this approach. Russell has gone down in the record books as one of the best basketball players who ever lived. But he was only mediocre in high school. He was considered mediocre by his coach in college, even after he was breaking records. The problem was that Bill Russell did not play the way everybody told him he should play. He was a big guy who did not keep both feet on the floor, as big guys were supposed to do. In short, Russell was the first center who jumped, and in the process, he revolutionized basketball.

Bill Russell had a vision for how he could play the game. And he stuck to his guns. In spite of tremendous pressure to change, he did not surrender that vision. He let his performance speak for itself, and the rewards followed. He was a five-time NBA Most Valuable Player and a twelve-time All-Star center. He became the first Black coach in the NBA. And he never surrendered his principles, even when racists envious of his brilliance tried to bend his will. I suspect that Bill Russell had a mama like mine.

Whatever your game is—whatever your life's work is—listen to your inner voice and find out how you want to play. Practice being yourself. And stick to your principles. That is the path to creating your reality. What follow are true health, wealth, and happiness.

2 *Knowledge*

THE VALUE OF UNDERSTANDING YOUR PURPOSE

I have already confessed to being ambitious. Succeeding has always been really important to me, and that drive was reinforced by everyone around me. I am not saying there is anything wrong with ambition, as long as you understand what you are striving for and are guided by your principles. For me, it took thirty years to reconnect with the core values Mama had instilled in me and to understand real success.

Fittingly, it was another angel, Mrs. Ruth Norman, my high school English teacher, who helped me understand what Mama had taught me. In a 1983 national television interview that I did with her on *Tony Brown's Journal,* she read, in "Negro dialect," as she had so many times before in class, Langston Hughes's poem "Mother to Son":

> *Well, son, I'll tell you:*
> *Life for me ain't been no crystal stair.*
> *It's had tacks in it,*
> *And splinters,*
> *And boards torn up,*
> *And places with no carpet on the floor—*
> *Bare.*
> *But all the time*
> *I'se been a-climbin' on,*
> *And reachin' landin's,*
> *And turnin' corners,*
> *And sometimes goin' in the dark*
> *Where there ain't been no light.*
> *So boy, don't you turn back.*
> *Don't you set down on the steps*
> *'Cause you finds it's kinder hard.*
> *Don't you fall, now—*
> *For I'se still goin', honey,*
> *I'se still climbin',*
> *And life for me ain't been no crystal stair.*

Listening to Mrs. Norman read the poem in my old classroom at Garnet High School, I was filled with memories of Mama—forever "a-climbin' on." Life never was "no crystal stair" for her, but she masterfully and wisely played the hand she was dealt. One particular incident came to mind, and right there on camera, on that day in 1983, I had an epiphany—I finally understood what Mama had tried to communicate to me about knowledge one day when I was in the sixth grade.

At school, we had just gotten into an area of complicated mathematics. I was at the kitchen table doing my homework one evening, struggling to solve a perplexing equation. Mama was also at the table, finishing up some sewing. I tried hard but just could not figure out the answer, growing more and more frustrated. In desperation, I asked Mama if she could help me. She put down her work, sat next to me, and looked over the assignment. "Sonny Boy, usually I do just fine with numbers, but I don't know much about all these complicated formulas," she said, shaking her head.

Obviously irritated, I blurted out, "Well, can't you figure it out? You always tell me that I can do anything if I put my mind to it."

"That's right," Mama replied awkwardly, "but some things you just can't do without schooling." I knew I had hurt and embarrassed her. I had not meant to do it, but in my drive to succeed—to master the problem—I had made her feel inadequate. I don't care who you are, for your own child to tell you, even if not in so many words, that you do not measure up hurts in a special way. To this day, it grieves me to think that I had caused her such pain.

That evening, nothing more was said about the incident. Mama returned to her sewing and I to my math. When it was time for bed, she called me over, hugged me to her, gave me a kiss, and then, looking in my eyes, said, "Anthony, learning is a precious thing. Never forget that. But knowing how to use your learning the right way is even more important."

The epiphany I had in Mrs. Norman's classroom in 1983 was that with those words Mama had taught me the core value of knowledge, even though she did not have enough schooling to help me solve a math problem. By 1983, I had been a university professor at one White (Central Washington University) and two Black (Howard University and Federal City College, now the University of the District of Columbia) institutions and the founding dean of the School of Communications at Howard. I knew from experience that traditional education, although a valuable skill, has produced its share of fools who believe that knowledge is a goal in itself and that accumulated knowledge makes you wise enough to attain health, wealth, and happiness. Well, all that does is make you think that you have to get degrees and titles in order to succeed in life. You study and work hard, and in the end, all you have to show for it is a seal of approval from the Establishment and a gnawing feeling that you have missed your true calling, that you have not fulfilled your mission in life. (I read a study once that found that an overwhelming majority of medical doctors, if they had it to do over again, would not become doctors.)

Mama could have told some of the learned scholars that true knowledge—knowledge that guides us down the path to health, wealth, and happiness—is the knowledge of our purpose in life, of the special role we can play in the world and the special work that each of us is uniquely capable of doing.

In the 1983 interview, Mrs. Norman reminded me of a quotation by Henry Van Dyke that she used to recite to us students to explain that any honest labor we are tasked to perform is a blessing. Van Dyke, with a dash of elegance, put it this way:

> *Let me do my work from day to day,*
> *in field or forest, at the desk or loom,*
> *in roaring marketplace or tranquil room.*
> *Let me but find it in my heart to say*

when vagrant wishes beckon me astray,
this is my work, my blessing, not my doom.
Of all who live, I am that one by whom
this work can best be done in the right way.

"Find a vocation you love," Mrs. Norman would tell us, "something you are called to do." She quoted Bessie Stanley's "Success":

He has achieved success who has lived well,
laughed often, and loved much,
who has gained the respect of intelligent men
and the love of little children,
who has filled his niche and accomplished his task,
who has left the world better than he found it.

Investing Your Talents

Mrs. Norman put it into words for us, gave us beautiful quotations and ideas to help us understand, but it was the whole community that taught us about success and character. We were taught that it was our responsibility to succeed, not only for ourselves but for the Black community as a whole. And the only way up was through education. The opportunity to learn was a privilege, one that would allow us to make a contribution to uplifting our people. Every adult in our environment reinforced that message. Even the wino on the corner would tell you, "I'm a failure. I'm a drunk. Don't be like me. Go to school."

Character building was an explicit part of our Norman Rockwell community of dark-skinned people. If we did not help one another—we were truthfully taught—there was no one else who would help us. Most adults felt an obligation to make sure that as young Blacks we benefited from their experience. In Charleston, if we children were on a public bus and were making noise, any Black adult had the authority to tell us to lower the volume, and we would comply. They were our elders and our role models, and we respected them. It was like a big extended family, and every part of the family reinforced the core values. And the most important value was to be mindful of the greater good.

This was not unique to Charleston. Regard for the greater good was always a part of the traditional values of the Black community. It was always a part of the ethos. Listen carefully to what most Black people are saying today and you will detect this core value of service.

The implicit message about knowledge I received while growing up was that everyone has something to contribute and that you have to find your niche. Work hard to discover what it is that you have to contribute to the greater good, we were taught, and then work even harder to make your contribution. The closest Mama came to formal instruction in communicating this message was with her favorite book, the Bible, and the biblical parables she loved so much.

One of them was the Parable of the Talents.[1] It is the story of a wealthy man who, before traveling to a distant land, entrusted his fortune to three servants. He gave five talents (a talent was a very large sum of money at that time) to one, two talents to another, and one to the third—"to every man according to his several ability."

Both the man who received five talents and the one who received two talents invested them and doubled the value of the fortunes with which they had been gifted. The man who received one talent was afraid of losing it and buried it in the earth. When their master returned, he rewarded the servants who had multiplied their wealth (their talents), but he punished the servant who did not invest (multiply) his talent, by taking the talent away and giving it to someone who would invest it in other people.

"Take the talent from him and give it to the one who has the ten talents," the master said, then cast the man of no works out of his household. "For unto every one who hath shall be given, and he shall have abundance: but from him that hath not shall be taken away even that which he hath. And cast ye the unprofitable servant into outer darkness." When this parable is understood as a life lesson for doing good works, it is obvious that it is intended for atheists as well as the faithful believers.

We were taught by our entire community that all of us had talents—intrinsic wealth—and that it was our duty to invest those talents to create wealth—social capital—for our community. Racism might keep us out of some jobs, but that did not mean we should not strive to achieve our most ambitious dreams. We might be temporarily without enough money to pay the rent, but that did not mean we could not afford to share our food with a neighbor who was hungry. To recognize your spiritual wealth and to share it "profitably," we were instructed, is an essential responsibility of being human.

Mrs. Norman used to quote to us a passage from James Russell Lowell on giving and sharing:

> Not that which we give, but what we share,—
> For the gift without the giver is bare;
> Who bestows himself with his alms feeds three,—
> Himself, his hungering neighbor, and me.

In our 1983 interview, Mrs. Norman also elaborated on the values she worked so hard to instill in us: "Love plus knowledge equals growth. So one of the things that I would always do is get myself together to stand up before you all, because I realized I was a role model. [She was critical of the dress code of today's teachers.] And the same thing about speech. . . . Through the years, Tony, I have filled my mind with beautiful thoughts of great minds and of the Bible, and I've shared these thoughts with thousands of students.

"When I was teaching at Stonewall Jackson [a formerly all-White high school where she taught after so-called integration closed Garnet] at every baccalaureate ceremony, the minister of the Bree Memorial Church here in Charleston would say to the graduates: 'You are somebody. But it all depends on you, what your goals are, what you're going to do. It's up to you whether you go up or down.'

"And the point is," Mrs. Norman concluded with a quote of another literary giant, John Oxenham, in "The Ways":

> *To every man there openeth*
> *A way and ways and a way.*
> *And the high soul climbs the high way,*
> *And the low soul gropes the low.*
> *And in between, on the misty flats,*
> *The rest drift to and fro.*
> *But to every man there openeth*
> *A high way and a low,*
> *And every man decideth*
> *The way his soul shall go.*

That message surrounded us—in school, in church, at home, out on the street. Mrs. Norman helped us develop knowledge through language and literature. Our parents and other adults built our knowledge by teaching us how to cope with life, how to deal with other people, and how to succeed by leaving this world a little better than we found it. The whole community invested its talents in us and in our development of knowledge.

Knowledge in the Eye of the Storm

Mama taught me to have knowledge of myself—to accept myself as equal—but never to think that I was better than anyone else. "Even if there are things that you do better than certain other people," she said, "don't get a big head and think that you're better than those people. Because every one of them can do something better than you can."

Mama also taught me that true knowledge is gained through overcoming adversity. "Find the center of the storm," she would tell me when things went wrong. "Don't resist. And let yourself be changed for the better. Some things are meant to happen."

I was headstrong, and this was not an easy lesson for me to learn. Too much pain, I thought. No thanks. However, Mama always found a way to share her wisdom with me to help me get the point. There is one particular incident that stands out in my memory. I was about ten years old. The circus was in town, and I desperately wanted to go. Mama would not let me, and I was steaming mad. I walked the floor and paced from room to room, banging things as I went along. I huffed and muttered. Mama sat very quietly in her chair, knitting and ignoring my temper tantrum. Finally, I stopped by the window with my back to her.

"I'm going to go and live with my mother," I threatened. "You're not my mother, anyway." I was very hostile, very mean at that moment. I still had this self-centeredness about me, as children often do at that immature and egoistic stage of development.

Mama remained silent and unperturbed. So I kept muttering about running away from home. She waited for me to simmer down. Then, after a few more minutes, Mama quietly put down her knitting, went into another room, and came back with a large brown paper bag. She set it down beside me on the floor and said, "You'll probably need some things for your trip."

Suddenly, I did not know what to do. I was immobilized. I was just broken down by her love at that moment. I stood there, seemingly for an eternity, staring straight ahead. Finally I meekly took the bag into another room and solemnly sat there by myself. Mama followed shortly and consoled me, as I had hoped she would.

I thought of this moment years later when I interviewed General Daniel "Chappie" James—the first Aframerican U.S. Air Force four-star general and member of the legendary Tuskegee Airmen, "America's Black Air Force," during World War II. He was talking about his mother and the role she had played in his life. "My mama had lots of sayings," he said in a big, husky voice. "My favorite has always been: 'When you knock on the door of opportunity and that door flies open, don't say you've got to go and pack your bags. Step in and take charge.'" General James and I hit it off when we first met and were friends for years, probably because we shared Mama experiences.

Mama did not just preach, she also lived by the values she taught me. Although it was clear that she was in a perennial struggle just to make ends meet, she never said we were poor. What we lacked in money, we made up for in optimism, hope, and pride. With enough work and enough study and enough working together, we would overcome and create a better situation. That is why I never developed a poverty or victim mentality—Mama did not believe in them. She believed in the goodness of the world, and she believed in me. This legacy has proved more valuable than money could ever be.

When I was a child, I never knew of a Black family in Charleston that received welfare benefits, no matter how poor they were. Welfare was reserved for poor White people. I remember Mama getting a sack of potatoes here, some surplus butter there. But there was no check every two weeks, or anything like the government paying your rent or buying your clothes or free school lunches. We would have been middle-class Blacks in Charleston had there been welfare for us.

Mama worked at whatever jobs she could get. She was a maid. She took day jobs, as they were called at the time. I do not know if she went through an agency or was referred from one family to another. Mostly, I remember meeting her at the bus stop after work. Once, I went on the bus with her to a very affluent White neighborhood, and she showed me a few of the houses where she had worked. I also visited her at the hotel where she worked as a dishwasher for a while.

Mama was at the low end of the Black female labor pool. In Charleston, if Black girls who had graduated from high school were light-skinned and pretty enough, they had a chance to get a job driving an elevator in one of the important office buildings. That was as far as they could go. Many of the girls succeeded as typist-secretaries in government jobs in Washington, D.C., because of Garnet's excellent vocational training program for those who were not on the college-preparation track. Black men could get better-paying jobs. Waiters did well. If you learned a trade, you could be an automobile repairman or an electrician. There was a handful of Blacks who could get jobs at the post office. But without a formal education, you were consigned to menial work, when you could get it. Unskilled Black women were at the bottom of this racist and sexist pecking order.

Frankly, to this day, I do not know how Mama did it. It was all magical to me. She just eked out a few dollars here and a few dollars there. And yet, she always seemed to have enough for the things I needed or wanted. I was the first boy on our block with a wagon. I had more comic books and marbles than any boy on the block. I was in the high school band and taking expensive music lessons in the fourth grade. But Mama did not simply spoil me. She also taught me the value of work.

At home, I had responsibilities. I had to clean up after myself. I had to wash dishes. I had to carry out the garbage. I had to help clean the house. I had to help with the shopping and other chores. Mama would let me help make her secret-formula "home brew," which she sold to earn extra money. She taught me about being a part of a team and working to make sure that I got what I wanted.

When I was old enough, I shined shoes after school at a shoe repair shop downtown; the White customers often rubbed my head for luck. During the summer, I drove an elevator and cleaned the bathrooms in a third-rate hotel for Whites only. I worked seven days a week, twelve hours a day, for ten dollars a week. Still later, while in high school, I worked as a busboy at what was formerly called the Daniel Boone Hotel, the city's tops.

Mama's message to me was consistent: Escape this way of life by finishing high school and going to college. The better I was in school, the better my chances would be of going to college and of getting a good job. I wanted to succeed, and I worked hard. It was very gratifying for me to have Mrs. Norman acknowledge this in the 1983 interview. She said, "Longfellow on work. I like this. 'The heights'—Tony, this reminds me of you. Longfellow says,

> *The heights by great men reached and kept*
> *Were not attained by sudden flight,*
> *But they while their companions slept*
> *Were toiling upward in the night."*

I felt so proud to hear Mrs. Norman say that to me because I knew I had followed Mama's advice. "If something is hard," she said, "don't give up, try even harder." Mama taught me that throughout life there would be bad times—crises necessary to change things for the better. "Anthony," she would say to me, repeating an old saying, "whatever doesn't kill you will make you stronger." This conviction came from her faith in God, and I have relied on Mama's faith all of my life to find knowledge at the center of the storm. Often, the callers to my radio talk show on WLS in Chicago refer to me as "the voice of reason." I know at those moments that I have a new brother or sister because Mama has resonated with the caller—Mama was in the house.

I had occasion to see the wisdom of Mama's advice as I was gathering material for this book last year. One afternoon I got a call from Jim Cannady, one of my closest friends and colleagues. Jim is one of the most knowledgeable multimedia and information technology experts in the country. He and I met when he was my student at Howard University. He has worked with me as an employee since he graduated in 1974.

Jim sounded as if he was under a lot of stress. His speech was halting and uncharacteristically unsure. Something was obviously wrong. As it turned out, Jim had been offered a significant post in a very well-funded information technology project of national significance. He was conflicted because of our loyalty to each other and my almost total dependence on him in our technology projects and the production of *Tony Brown's Journal* on PBS.

As I listened to his plea to help him resolve this situation, I was flooded with fear. It seemed that chaos was about to descend into my life. Since the job was in another city, I would be losing not only Jim but also his wife, Sheryl, who has been my producer and close friend since 1972. After the shock subsided, I followed Mama's advice of seeking knowledge in the eye of the storm. The fear and chaos gave way to the clarity of a higher consciousness. I realized and focused on how much I loved—not needed—Jim and Sheryl. And with that I could see what a wonderful opportunity this was for both of them.

I pointed out to Jim that he would earn nearly twice as much money and would have a major role in shaping the future of our nation's place in the new millennium, and with the prospect of financing the college tuition of his twelve-year-old son looming, the added security would be just what the doctor ordered. We also discussed the fact that Jim would be the only Aframerican in such a sensitive position. Black people would have a much-needed champion in information technology. (As it turned out, Sheryl would soon join Jim at the same bureau.)

How could the success and happiness of two of my best friends possibly adversely affect me? I love my friends and, as I know from Mama, what is good for them is ultimately good for me. I said all this to Jim, and his guilt about abandoning a friend was alleviated by my truth. I would offer my support and, of course, give him the highest recommendation. Jim and I left the phone conversation with a stronger love and respect for each other than ever before.

When Jim's prospective new boss called for a reference, he and I hit it off very well. We both had enough expertise in the field and enough common sense to know how fortunate he was to find a gem like Jim. And since we were in related areas and had many shared interests, Jim's new boss suggested that we might explore some joint projects. Mama was right again: It is exactly in the most turbulent places that we can gain true knowledge of ourselves—knowledge that helps us achieve health, wealth, and happiness. When you know and play your role in serving the greater good, you create harmony, real capital, and joy.

Putting Knowledge to Work

One of Yogi Berra's sayings—and the title of his 2001 book—is, "When you come to a fork in the road, take it." Mama's advice had a similar sly wisdom. She prepared me for the fact that just when you think you are walking down a well-defined path, either something will force you into another path or the path itself will be transformed right under your feet. She taught me to embrace the unexpected and to learn from it. How to do that was up to me.

The lesson was: There are no operating instructions for life. I was expected to go to college, for example, but I had to figure out for myself that, in order to go to college, I had to get out and earn money to pay my tuition and living expenses. Every obstacle I encountered, I had to learn to deal with on my own. What I did not have laid the foundation for what I would learn.

My experience with college is a prime example of the significant disparity in opportunity that existed in this country in the 1950s. After qualifying academically without any assistance from race-based entitlement programs, I was still poor, Black, and with no parents to support me. There was no financial aid, no loans, and no programs to promote equity in higher education in this era of unequal opportunity. Making the task more daunting, Wayne tacked on an "out-of-state" charge because I was not a resident of Michigan. People like me were systematically and consistently shut out of college.

It was only because of Mama and my upbringing that I valued a college education enough to be willing and able to make the sacrifices necessary to work my way through school, that I persevered in facing the challenges essentially alone. Before you are tempted to feel sorry for this poor, disadvantaged "minority" (a term I disdain), you should realize that the fact that I managed to get a college education in spite of all the factors that conspired against me gave me the added advantage of knowing that I was resourceful enough to make it in the real world.

And because of this success and a head full of Mama's beautiful ideas, I have triumphed over neglect and racism, and I am not angry with anyone. Every challenge, Mama said, is an opportunity in disguise. "The more you are challenged, the more you will learn and grow and the more you will succeed." In fact, I am thankful that circumstances forced me to discover that I possess what Germans call *Arbeitswut,* a fury for work, and an abiding belief in the principle known as the Privilege of Labor. It holds that any honest work is a blessing from God. I guess you could say that I stared adversity in the face and beat it back with faith and fury.

In Detroit, as a Southern immigrant, I had to get used to a

whole different culture. And it was the Black people, as much as the White people, who surprised me. Although I had once lived in a poor neighborhood by Charleston standards, I had never seen slums like Detroit's before. I had never seen so many Black people live the way they lived in Detroit's racial ghettos, or dress the way they dressed, or use drugs. I had never seen rich Black people before, either. There were a few well-off Blacks in Charleston, but in Detroit I encountered truly rich Blacks. One man owned an island, replete with his own thoroughbred horses. When his daughter got married, he spent more money on the wedding than most people earned in five years in those days.

Of course, the biggest difference was that Charleston was a small town, with a population of fifty thousand and five thousand Blacks. Detroit was a city of about half a million, with a Black population of 15 to 20 percent. And, as in most Northern cities, Blacks and Whites in Detroit talked about equality, but they rarely got around to practicing it. Deep down, there was no love lost. In Charleston, although we lived separately, there were relationships that were more socially intimate than what I saw up North. America is truly a racial paradox.

The biggest challenge for me was adapting to competing academically with White people, in a White institution. Psychologically, that required moving directly into the center of the storm. I had to contend with one of the implicit lessons of segregation, that Blacks were getting an inferior education because we were separated from Whites. This, of course, is a racist view.

The quality of academic education is not determined by the mix of ethnic groups in the classroom. You are not automatically harmed if you learn with people of your own ethnicity. You are harmed only if you do not learn to respect yourself, if you do not learn to love yourself. You cannot respect or love a person from another group unless you have first learned to respect and love yourself. Being with people just because they are different misses the point. Self-respect and mutual respect are the crucial issues.

I went to a school that was all Black. The teachers were Black and the students were Black. (But we were taught principles that are universal.) We were given an excellent basic education. There was nothing in our education that taught us that White people were inferior or superior. Therefore, I never learned either myth formally. Nevertheless, the racist Establishment system unconsciously eroded my confidence in Black institutions, and when I got to college I had to deal with feelings of insecurity about being able to compete with White students.

I remember, the very first class I had was German. This was my first day at Wayne. There must have been twenty or more students in the class, and I was the only Black person. As we walked into the classroom and took our seats, many of my fellow students greeted the professor in what sounded to me like German. He answered them, and they seemed to be able to carry on a conversation. Well, you can imagine my state of mind. First day of class, and I am already behind the eight ball. All the racial myths just came tumbling down on me: Whites are smarter. They are better prepared. All this fear because I just got the book and these guys are already speaking German.

This was September, and during the month there were several Jewish holidays in a row. I did not know anything about Jewish holidays at that time. I went to class one day, and there were maybe four people in the room. I asked where everyone was. "Well, this is a Jewish holiday," one of my classmates explained. It did not take me long to realize that the vast majority of the class was Jewish. I also learned that many Jews speak Yiddish, a combination of German and Hebrew. That was how the Jewish students could communicate with the professor on the first day of class.

I learned a lot from that initial reaction, though. I recognized in myself the unconscious fear that I could not cut the mustard among White people. To counteract that fear, I studied harder. And I did fairly well. I got a B out of the class, the happiest B I had ever received in my life, and became one of the hard-nosed professor's favorite students. My ability to make decent grades and earn acceptance helped me overcome the fear and build my confidence.

I also learned that the greatest value of desegregation is the opportunity to get to know people from other cultures, so you do not rely on stereotypes to understand individual behavior. Not only do you learn to appreciate different cultures but, more important, you learn to judge people on the basis of their character and not their group identity. And it is when you engage with individuals that you begin to see through the evil mythology of racism.

College was also the place where I started to acquire some real knowledge about my calling in life. I did not know then what form it would take, but I started to realize that I wanted to speak on behalf of my community. It was a time during which I became increasingly aware socially and politically. One experience was of particular importance in this awakening.

I took a class in economics. On the first day of class, after taking attendance and briefly staring at me, the professor asked me to stand up. "You are Mr. Brown?" he inquired. "I would like for you to consider dropping this course." Just like that, in front of the whole class. No reason given, no reason needed. Everyone could see that he assumed that, as the only Black student, I would be incapable of understanding the law of supply and demand or vertical integration.

At that moment, I wanted the floor to open up and swallow me, or to wake up from what, I hoped, must be a nightmare. I sat down, trembling, humiliated, and unable to respond. Some of the White students seemed embarrassed. I remember little else of that class. I was in shock. This was as bad as anything that had ever happened to me in Charleston, in the South.

I was tempted to drop the course, mostly to avoid further embarrassment and out of fear that the professor would deliberately flunk me, but I decided that I was not going to give in as my fear turned into anger and determination. I relied on Mama's teaching about gaining knowledge from adversity to get me through. I figured that the best way to get back at this guy would be to do well. So I spent day and night studying economics. In the process, I discovered that I love the subject.

I have always been blessed with an exceptional memory, and I took copious notes. When it came time to take our first exam, an essay test, I filled several blue books, quoting the lectures almost word for word. The following week, before returning our blue books, the professor said in his thick European accent, "Mr. Brown, would you stand." Mustering every ounce of courage I had left, I stood up and braced myself for the worst. I was still worried that he would find a way to fail me simply because of his antipathy toward Blacks.

"I would like to apologize to you before the class," the professor announced amid a stunned silence. "You have written one of the best papers I have ever read." (This was another lesson about succeeding in college: Don't try to be original; just regurgitate the professor's theories about the subject.) He went on to say that he hoped I would remain as one of his students. Ironically, he and I became guarded friends, and to this day I respect him for having the integrity to offer that public apology. It takes a person of strong character to recognize and make amends for one's prejudices.

This was one of the real milestones in my life, having stood up to this man. And it was also the beginning of my activism. I became convinced that I could make a difference, that I could challenge racism, and that I could make things better. I knew that through my actions I had made the path a little easier for other Black students. I became self-empowered. I knew that I could change this society, that my ideas and my voice could be heard. I was certainly going to try. I also knew that I had to be persistent, I had to keep going into the turbulence.

The next ordeal was a very different one. This was my first time away from home. I wanted and needed friends and a support network. I needed some love from Black people to help me cope with the constant racist turbulence. Pledging a fraternity seemed like the answer to my needs. So I went to the smokers, the recruiting parties. My ambition drove me to seek out the very best on campus, to see if I could make it among them. Each fraternity laid out a good case, but the one that really impressed me was Alpha Phi Alpha. I remember the recruitment pitch that told me Alpha was the place for me: Every president of every Black college, at that time, was an Alpha. My impression was that they were the best academically and the most socially connected.

Alpha Phi Alpha was the first Black "Greek" fraternity. ("Pelasgian" is the correct name for unassimilated native Greeks who were Afro-Asiatic in appearance. For more about this, see my book *Black Lies, White Lies*.) It was founded by seven brilliant Black male students (Jewels) in 1906 at Cornell University. Hundreds of thousands of Black male college students, including such luminous "brothers" as Martin Luther King, Jr., have since become Alphas for life.

There was a definite element of elitism, not just in Alpha, but in the entire Black Greek world at that time. Alpha Phi Alpha said fraternities want only the best, and it was the best fraternity. Alpha preferred highly motivated overachievers and socioeconomic elitists. Here I was, a poor outsider with egalitarian leanings, seeking turbulence again. Lucky for me, my academic standing and high energy level made me acceptable as an Alpha pledge.

In those days, you had to serve a sort of hazing internship to be eligible to be admitted into the fraternity. So, I joined Alpha's pledge branch, the Sphinx Club. I was a Sphinxman for a year, an unusually long and brutal period. (It would have been shorter had I not tried to throw a big brother who was harassing me out of an eighth-floor dormitory window.) When I look back on it, I cannot believe that I subjected myself to the psychological and physical abuse, but at the time I really wanted to prove myself.

We were paddled every week, on Sunday mornings, and sometimes during the week as well. Huge guys just whaling away at you with all their might with sturdy pieces of wood. I shudder to think of the dangers of it. In addition, there was the psychological "discipline," as it was called. We had to address the fraternity men as Big Brother. We had to be subservient. They would show off in front of the girls, ordering us around: "Go get my shoes. Go get me something to eat. Clean off my table." There were also constant history tests and academic evaluations.

It was partly an endurance program, but I was determined to become an Alpha. I was even elected president of the Sphinx Club. There were about fifty of us who started out, and only four who finished. (Before my time, the great Jackie Robinson, an outstanding scholar and the first Black to play baseball in the major leagues, was a failed Sphinxman.) These three survivors (dogs) of my "line," in addition to myself, included Dr. George Shirley, who debuted on October 24, 1961, as the first Aframerican principal tenor (as opposed to chorus member) engaged by the Metropolitan Opera; Dr. Dalmas Taylor, a psychologist who later became the dean of the College of Liberal Arts at Wayne State University; and James Rucker, a prominent Detroit lawyer.

Alpha Phi Alpha had a lot to do with our success and was well worth the effort. Everything I endured was worth learning: humility, "manly deeds, scholarship, and love for all mankind"—the Alpha creed. Fraternities and sororities created tremendous benefits for a few. Unfortunately, many young Black men and women were psychologically traumatized by rejection from Greek letter organizations. The popularity of elitism, along with its emphasis on being light-skinned, among Blacks has gone the way of the dodo bird, as has the useless brutality. As we grow out of self-hatred and into self-empowerment, we learn to love everyone as an equal.

At that time, however, the Alpha way was the "best" or nothing at all. Everyone in the fraternity was an academic overachiever. Out of a chapter with a membership of fifty undergraduates, about half of the brothers were premedical students and about 80 percent of them, as I recall, had a cumulative grade point average of between 3.5 (B+) and 4.0 (A). Unfortunately, according to rumors, at that time, Wayne State's medical school accepted only one Black and seven Jews each year for its freshman class of one hundred. The one-Black quota was shared by every Black person in the world, not just my fraternity chapter, Alpha Upsilon, or other Blacks at Wayne.

Some of these overqualified (by today's standards) men became schoolteachers because they could not get into medical school. Others became scientists, optometrists, and pharmacists. A quota based on discrimination kept them from pursuing their dreams. This injustice reinforced my indignation at the unfairness of the system. Even when you played by the rules and exceeded all qualifications, discrimination was there waiting to keep you out. Ironically, although I joined Alpha Phi Alpha mainly to gain status, what I ended up gaining was a deeper knowledge of myself and a more informed social consciousness of serving my community.

At that time, the fraternity was not involved enough in the social and political movements of the day, but little by little I was being transformed. I was very angry about the injustices I saw. They went against everything I had learned, and I was now in a position to give voice to my new awareness. I was no longer a little boy in Charleston, where I had to remain passive. I now had awareness, had knowledge—and, despite racism, had greatly expanded opportunity.

Alpha Phi Alpha, in many ways, was the single most important factor in my transition into manhood. I put that experience on a par with my experience in the Army. These were really transformative events in my life. They were places where I honed my knowledge—I threw myself headlong into the turbulence and emerged with a clearer sense of myself and my purpose.

As my awareness grew, I moved away from the fraternity and toward involvement in the community. Once I graduated and began writing for the *Detroit Courier,* I had a public forum, and that identity grew stronger. That is when I really started finding out where I was going to end up in life.

For me today, television is a form of community activism (see

Empowerment Television in Chapter five). I represent the community. I do not represent any television network or station or news organization. I represent the best interests of the community. I started out representing the best interests of the Black community. Today, I represent the best interests of our total community. I have grown and continue to grow with the world, and I define my community as all people who share my core values and my interests. My knowledge has become deeper and wider, and every day I am grateful for the opportunity to continue to serve the greater good.

I am going to end this chapter with the Pavlovian technique employed by Mrs. Norman at the end of every class. Precisely when the bell rang, she would say: "So much to learn, and so little time to learn it in." But there is time enough to learn what your true calling in life is, to gain knowledge of what it is that you have to contribute to the greater good. That knowledge is the only viable path to health, wealth, and happiness.

Humanity

THE VALUE OF BEING ONE RACE, THE HUMAN RACE

On June 23, 1963, in Detroit's Cobo Hall, I listened to Martin Luther King, Jr., deliver his famous "I Have a Dream" speech, for what many claim was the first time. Dr. King was in Detroit for the Walk to Freedom march that I had coordinated. I was on the stage with the other organizers, looking out at the overflowing audience, drinking in the soul-stirring words.

I knew that I was passionately committed to tearing down the injustice of America's racist society. On that day in 1963, I discovered the source of that passion.

"I have a dream my four little children will one day live in a nation where they will not be judged by the color of their skin but by the content of their character. I have a dream today!" Dr. King proclaimed. And at that moment I felt a profound shock of recognition. I knew the terrible unfairness of color-based judgment, but it was not only racist Whites who inflicted it on me, it was also my own community, even my own family. In fact, it was from the Browns that I first learned how the poisonous mythology of racism had infected the minds of Aframericans.

My parents were from different sides of the color "tracks"—my father, Royal Brown, was very light-skinned (from a family of Halle Berry phenotypes, but with fairer skin), and my mother, Catherine Davis, was very dark, with prominent and beautiful African and Native American features. The Browns, a leading Black Charleston family, deeply disapproved of the match and did their utmost to keep the young couple apart. My parents never married but did have five children, whose skin color spanned the whole spectrum. After my father abandoned her, my distraught mother farmed us children out to a variety of family members, neighbors, and, in my case, strangers. (Mama had had no previous connection with my family.)

Although my siblings and I all lived separately, we knew that we were a family. We played together, celebrated birthdays and holidays together, helped one another out. It was printed indelibly on our psyches, as a source of pride, that we were Browns. When we spent time with the Browns, however, it was clear that they divided us into the Browns and the Davises, based on our color. The Brown-colored were treated like family, the Davis-colored like barely tolerated interlopers. It was so unfair, and nearly impossible for a child to understand. But this color-consciousness was the reality of the Black community everywhere at that time.

Unfortunately, the seeds of White colonialism still grow into the insidious weeds of self-hatred, wherever they are planted. Across the vast continent of Africa, the popularity of skin-lightening cream (resplendent with ingredients that "can increase the likelihood of skin cancer" and mercury-induced blotches on even darker skin) among "a Black population in the hundreds of millions" seems "most absurd."[1] This negative legacy is especially hard on dark women who are trying to please African men (whom they need economically). The dilemma of not loving oneself always leads to an overreliance on others, in this case on what men think. These African men are not even in love with White women; they neurotically chase the unattainable object because it is not black.

The self-involved not-as-rich-as-he-once-was zillionaire Michael Jackson, whose career, a record executive was quoted as saying, has crashed because of allegations and rumors of pedophilia, sings that it doesn't matter if you're Black or White. But that Neverland rhetoric is belied by the truth that he manages to look whiter and whiter every time he lowers his mask in public. A white Negro. What is also obvious is his opportunistic use of the race card. He uses the Black issue as both a sword and a shield.

It seems logical to conclude that we are witnessing an ethnically challenged incognegro exploit the principle of color blindness as a shield when he wants to con Whites into buying his music and as a sword when he plays the race card to exploit naïve Blacks and mobilize opportunistic Blacks who provide His Whiteness with a general-waiver C.Y.A. from the imperatives of self-respect and integrity. In truth, his goal is millions more from the White record executives who oppose his manipulative tactics and greed.

To Michael Jackson's dubious slur that a White man with two ex-wives (one Jewish and one Black) and a current wife who is Mexican, Sony executive Tommy Motolla, is a racist, comedian

Robin Williams quipped, "Michael, you've got to pick a race first." But the Gary, Indiana, Black boy has chosen to disguise himself as His Whiteness. His true identity is unknown to most of us, probably even to himself, and it is likely to remain a mystery because a possible self-loathing rejects the true reality of how beautiful he was as himself.

Another example may further demonstrate what I mean when I say that the main problem of Aframericans is the racial self-hatred we were forced to incorporate into our personalities during slavery and legal segregation that was passed down from generation to generation. Millie McGhee has published a book (*Secrets Uncovered: J. Edgar Hoover—Passing for White?*, Allen-Morris, 2000) about her long-held family secret that the man known to the world as J. Edgar Hoover (and clandestinely as "Mary," his alleged homosexual nom de guerre), the FBI's infamous and authoritarian director, had his origins in her Pike County, Mississippi, Black family. According to McGhee and widespread rumors, Hoover the Aframerican "passed" after moving to Washington, D.C., via the special underground railroad for mulatto Blacks who planned to pass for White in the North. McGhee also told me this story on *Tony Brown's Journal*.

Gore Vidal, the writer, who also grew up in Washington, D.C., is quoted as saying that "it was always said of him—in my family and around the city—that he was a mulatto."[2] Among Blacks in the East, Hoover was often referred to as a "spook" (slang for Black).[3]

If all or some of these allegations are true, Hoover's extreme racism and obsession with destroying Black leaders may have been a diversionary tactic to avoid being discovered as a Black man, and on another level, it would have been a psychological defense mechanism to manage his painful and hateful perception of his African ancestry.

In other words, severe bigotry and resentment of his Black identity could have been an unhealthy adaptation to his alleged Black bloodline that was projected onto other Blacks, such as Martin Luther King, whom Hoover referred to as "the biggest liar" in the country. Examine that statement in the context of Hoover's projection of his own unconscious fears and feelings—about himself. That is so tragic.

Both His Whiteness and "Mary," alter egos, are tragic figures of the terrible psychological burden that America's obsession with white supremacy has had on Aframericans who did not have a mama like mine who instilled human dignity. I feel sorry for any Black person who goes through life and fails to discover how beautiful it is to be Black. There are millions of Black people (physically Caucasian in phenotype) who are passing for White. Carol Channing (*Hello Dolly*), for example, waited until she was eighty-one to tell the world that she is Aframerican (according to the blood rule of hypo descent) in her autobiography *Just Lucky I Guess*. Hello, Dolly Black! I was spared any such doubts because Mama knew why the original beauty in everyone is special.

Family

"Just like you and your brothers and sisters are one family, we're all God's children, no matter what color" was Mama's antidote to the mental cancer of self-hatred among Africans and Aframericans who believe that lighter equals prettier. "People are foolish not to love one another, Anthony," she would say to me when I complained to her about some color injustice at the Browns. Small wonder that in 1963, as I listened to Dr. King finish his first "Dream" speech in Detroit, I thought of Mama.

It began to come together for me at that moment. The core value Mama had taught me about race was that there is only one race—the human race. Dr. King's words helped me understand the profound meaning of Mama's teaching: It is your humanity that determines your value as a person. And if you value your humanity, no one can stand in your way to health, wealth, and happiness.

The Mythology of Race

The Browns were in no way unique in their attitudes about race. In fact, they were typical of a society that used skin color as a primary criterion for evaluating a person's abilities, potential, and worth. For hundreds of years, all symbols of goodness were white. If you were given a little White "goodness," society—including members of your own community—saw you in a whole different light. When I went to school, the pretty light-skinned girls were often placed in the front row. Few of them ever got a failing grade. Some Black colleges required a photograph with your application; they wanted to see whether you were light or dark. Black men fought over light-skinned women, but if you were a dark-skinned woman, rejection was more likely. W. E. B. Du Bois's so-called Talented Tenth elitist Blacks, who were light-skinned as a rule, institutionally separated themselves from the Black masses they purported to lead.

This was the paradox that we lived with. We were taught to believe that we could be somebody if we worked hard enough, and implicitly, we were taught that it would be a whole lot easier for those of us who were light-skinned and had White features to become somebody.

I learned the power of this paradox at the hands of Robert Atkins, a classmate when we were small boys who later became a close friend. One day after school, Robert attacked me and gave me a pretty bad drubbing. A little while later, after my bruised ego had recovered a bit, I went up to him and asked, "Why did you beat me up?" And with absolute sincerity, Robert, who was darker than I am, said, "Because you are the only light-skinned guy I know who has bad hair." By "bad hair" he meant that I have Black hair.

I would not have been able to articulate this at the time, but it was this distortion of how Black people treated one another that made me the angriest about racism. Sure, I got angry when the White boys would call me nigger. I became angry when I saw that the system was rigged to keep me from winning.

I will never forget, for example, the frustration I felt as a paperboy. There was a White guy, Rollins, who was my archrival. We were both very competitive, so we admired the hell out of each other and fought all the time to be the best. You had to run to get to your customers first. Rollins and I were the two fastest guys there. He would win one night; I would win the next night. But when it came down to it, Rollins was always given the edge, because he was White. I knew that I had to beat him in spite of his having that edge. I knew it was unfair, but I had learned from Mama that the best way to beat the system was to be good enough to win. "Nothing succeeds like success," I was taught.

Although I did not like it, I could accept that the White people in Charleston did not want to live with us or give us jobs. (There seemed to be a conspiracy to run Blacks out of Charleston.) What I could not accept, as I understood later, was getting beaten up by a Black guy because my hair was too African or having my father's Black family reject my biological mother because her skin was too dark. That was the most hurtful and unforgivable injustice, in my mind, of the racist system Whites had set up: It had taught Black people self-hatred.

Mama taught me that hatred was not only an absence of love but more an absence of faith, and self-hatred is the absence of faith in yourself. "If you believe in yourself," she would tell me, "you don't need to hate anybody, to look down on anybody. We are all God's children, just remember that."

Mama's faith in God was the source of her faith in people—even people who have no faith in themselves. And she saw the racist myth of superiority for what it is, a desperate attempt to relieve the spiritual pain that comes from self-hatred. People who are racist have no faith in themselves. Therefore, they resort to looking down on an entire group of people to make themselves feel less inadequate. Today, we call that a neurosis. Mama called it misguided and ungodly.

In fact, today there is scientific proof that Mama was right. Advances in genetics have shown that there is almost no variation in the DNA codes of humans, no matter what "race" we are. For example, the biological difference between Blacks and Whites amounts to a genetic sunburn. Only six genes out of as many as forty thousand determine skin color.[4] We are indeed all God's children, as Mama repeatedly said: We all trace our lineage not simply to common ancestors but to one set of human parents.

"I often say that America doesn't have a racial problem; it has a reasoning problem," Yehudi Webster, associate professor of sociology at California State University in Los Angeles, recently told *The Washington Post.*[5]

"It is disturbing to see reputable scientists and physicians even categorizing things in terms of race," concurs Dr. Joseph L. Graves, Jr., a noted professor of evolutionary biology and African-American studies at Arizona State University.[6] Dr. Graves, author of *The Emperor's New Clothes: Biology Theories of Race at the Millennium,* bluntly argues, in *The New York Times,* that "races do not exist and that race is simply a social and political construct that the world would be better without. Racism, he says, is fueled by the idea that human beings can be separated by genetics into races."

Dr. Graves asserts that although different groups of humans are "anatomically different from each other," "there is no subspecies," and "distinct lineages" are not possible, because "throughout history, we have had too much gene flow between so-called races." Miscegenation in Europe, Africa, and particularly in America has destroyed any possibility of "unique lineages," he adds. The United States created a "Black race" by classifying individuals by means of "the rule of hypodescent"—the rudely ignorant hypothesis "whereby one drop of black blood makes one Black," explains Dr. Graves.

In "The Tree of Me," a 2001 article in *The New Yorker,* John Seabrook presents definitive genetic evidence that we are all descendants of a single matrilineal family.[7] The article, which is subtitled "DNA Testing Is Revolutionizing the Field of Genealogy: Are We Ready for What We Might Find?," also makes it clear how invested we are in the unreal concept of race.

Seabrook wisely admonishes us about "the golden rule of the age of household genetics: Never ask for an answer you don't need to know." If you do ask, you may be confronted with a situation similar to the one that Dr. Rick Kittles, of Howard University, found himself in. In using DNA to trace his African ancestry, Kittles "discovered that he was part German on his father's side."[8] The irony is that Kittles's German ancestor's DNA can most likely be traced to African ancestors, at least on the mother's side, since all of us, if we are to believe our genetic material, come from one African mother in the Garden of Eden.

Archaeological evidence further supports the theory that all human life originated in Africa, or Alkebu-Lan, the "Garden of Eden" and "the Mother of Mankind," as it was known to its original inhabitants. The oldest fossils of human ancestors continue to come from Africa. The 3.5-million-year-old "Lucy" and the equally ancient "Kenyan flat-face," discovered in 2001, were both found in East Africa and are quite likely among the first representatives of our maternal line.

Even more recently (July 19, 2001), scientists found an African skull that dates the oldest fossil of a human ancestor ever in the cradle of civilization, Alkebu-Lan (Africa). Toumai ("hope of life"), as the fossil was named, lived in the sub-Saharan Sahel region of Chad, Africa, seven million years ago.[9] Toumai was from around the time "when the human and chimpanzee lineages went their separate ways"[10] and was an Afro-Asiatic ancestor of the likely colonizers of Europeans and their civilization, as well as the rest of the world.[11] It became a shock in scientific circles when one of those colonizers, now a 1.75-million-year-old fossil, turned up in Georgia during the same week Toumai was discovered in Chad.[12] "A skull in what used to be the Soviet Union may have belonged to one of the first human forerunners to make it out of Africa."[13]

Science has not only located our birthplace in Alkebu-Lan but has also begun to explain the dispersion of our species across the continents and our biological adaptation to a variety of climactic conditions. "Tracing Your Genetic Roots: DNA Mapping Is Unraveling the Mystery of Human Origins" ("Where We Come From"), a 2001 cover story in *U.S. News & World Report,* reported on DNA studies aimed at determining "the peopling of Europe."[14] One of the studies traced maternal DNA; the other traced paternal DNA. "These findings portray the majority of European forebears arriving from" northeast Africa (named the Middle East by Europeans and Americans after World War II), according to the scientists who conducted the research.[15]

About 50,000 years before wandering into Europe, the researchers maintain, Africans wandered into northeast Africa and Asia as the forebears of the Afro-Asiatics.[16] These African "hunter-gatherers" then went on to colonize Europe between 25,000 and 40,000 years ago, when they migrated from northeast Africa. These Black people who discovered the European continent were called the Grimaldi, and their unbroken stream of migrations over many centuries began at the Cape in South Africa, according to the author Mark Hyman.[17] Since there was no Strait of Gibraltar, the Grimaldi "walked on dry land and into Spain and France," while still others went into Italy and beyond.

As they settled in different climates, the Grimaldi Africans physically adapted to their environments. Over thousands of years, the original phenotype (physical characteristics) changed. In Northern Europe, where solar radiation is weakest, the need for melanin diminished and people's skin slowly became white. In a similar fashion, the nostrils became long and narrow, because in a cold climate the body needs a longer period of time to warm up the air before it gets to the lungs. Wherever our ancestors settled on their migration out of Africa, with time they developed physical characteristics best suited to the climate.

Generations of Black blues musicians have sung about leaving Chicago to return down South, to "where the weather suits my clothes." The reality is that humans have always suited themselves to the weather. Our physical features are nothing more than adaptations to climactic conditions.

"The mathematical study of genealogy indicates that everyone in the world is descended from Nefertiti and Confucius, and everyone of European ancestry is descended from Muhammad and Charlemagne."[18] In the same issue of *The Atlantic* that includes this statement, Steve Olson makes the case, based on the mathematical study of genealogy, that "almost everyone in the New World must be descended from English royalty—even people of predominantly African and Native American ancestry," because of the long history of intermarriage and miscegenation in the Americas.

The genes of all humans come from one African mama, "The Real Eve," according to experts on a Discovery Channel special.[19] We're all related to one woman—nicknamed Eve—who lived in East Africa more than 150,000 years ago.[20] We all share a genetic heritage through mitochondrial DNA that enables scientists to trace genetic lines back to a primordial source. Based on research and "scholarly concurrence," *The Wall Street Journal* concluded that "all non-Africans have their origins in a single East African woman."[21] There is a "powerful cultural—and political—message," according to the *Journal:* "We are one, and our differences are but skin deep."[22]

My mama, through her faith in God, knew this to be true all along, before science confirmed it with facts. She tried to teach me, and anyone else who would listen, that each person's value comes from his or her humanity, not their physical features. In the racially segregated Charleston, West Virginia, of my childhood, I found it difficult to really understand what she meant. And once she was gone and I became more conscious of the hatred, injustice, and oppression of institutional racism, I rebelled against what I considered the misguided sentimentality of her wisdom. After all, we were still riding in the back of the bus, both literally and figuratively, and we were still judging one another by the color of our skin. I came to see everything—people, issues, ideas—in black and white.

Fighting racism and the oppression of Blacks in this country became a personal mission. I did not discover that the foundation of this mission was Mama's belief in humanity until I heard Dr. King speak on that June day in 1963. Dr. King not only inspired me but also helped me rediscover Mama. (She always said that an "expert" is someone from out of town—with a briefcase.)

Racism and Self-Hatred

As with most other things Mama taught me, it took me decades to understand and accept her belief that there is only one race—the human race. Since the whole society was based on color and race, I just dismissed what Mama said as coming from her faith rather than a realistic understanding of the world. I am embarrassed to admit that this judgment was in part based on the fact that she was not formally educated. After all, I reasoned, Mama could not even help me with sixth-grade math.

I also rejected her assertion that Blacks should forgive White people. I could not see any reason why I should forgive Whites. They had created a system that was immoral and evil. I knew some wonderful people who were White, but I held some very deep-seated hostilities toward White people as a group.

Paradoxically, these feelings first came to the surface when I arrived in Detroit, a city that was not legally segregated. In Charleston, you knew where you were. Black people were here. White people were over there. That was how things were. It was not an angry place. The Black community was not angry; it was very complacent and accepting.

When I left the protective nest of Charleston's Aframerican community and entered Detroit's desegregated culture, I came face-to-face with White people not as an abstract group but as individuals. I was now with Whites in classrooms. I was with Whites in cafeterias. I was with Whites at parties, learning how to socialize and hold back from saying what you really feel and believe. I was with Whites in intellectual settings, where we were on equal footing, debating how to solve the problems of the world.

I was stopped on a regular basis by the White police, in many cases just because I am a Black male. "Someone who fits your description committed a crime," the cops would always say. But most of the time I was stopped because my girlfriend at the time was very light-skinned, and the police wanted to know what a White woman was doing with a Black man. With every incident, my sense of outrage at the injustice of racism grew.

Then I was drafted. When I returned to Detroit from the Army, I was twenty and had seen the world. I had lived in Europe for two years. I had been independent, and I was now a man. I had enough skills and maturity to realize that I could do something about the injustices I saw. I said, "Sure, Blacks can't work at the bank. We cannot be journalists. We can't buy homes on certain blocks. But I can do something about all this." My confidence and sense of empowerment began to emerge at this time. And I no longer felt that I had to hide and manage my anger.

TONY BROWN

Mama had trained me to manage my emotions, the way Black parents have done since Black men were born in this society. Putting a lighter spin on this cultural phenomenon, comedian Chris Rock commented on why he is glad that his wife had a girl: "I think I'd be too hard on a boy—every day, trying to make him a man, getting him ready for White people."[23]

This cultural adaptation is not unique to Aframericans. Wherever you find a persecuted group, the culture of that group traditionally protects those of its members who are most in danger by teaching them to be less aggressive. Black males have always been taught that you are feared, that you threaten Whites, particularly some White males, that you can come off as uppity very easily, and that lynchings were historically targeted at you. (Police profiling and sporadic beatings of Black males today prove the wisdom of this cultural adaptation in the face of society's intractable racist habits.)

In my day, it was essential for Black males to learn to be non-threatening. Often it was a matter of life and death. Shamefully, Black parents are still forced to teach their sons, if stopped by the police, to keep their hands in full sight and keep their voices low—and polite—no matter how unfair the harassment may seem.

Mama, like all Black parents, was intent on protecting me by teaching me how to be nonthreatening and compliant. The way she punished me was designed to teach me how to restrain my feelings and demonstrate submission to authority. The "Switch Dance" was our version of the cultural ritual of curbing assertive behavior as an adaptive survival pattern. (Most Aframerican institutions are survival institutions.)

We did the Switch Dance when I broke the rules. When I did something for which I deserved to be punished, Mama would tell me to go outside and pick the switches. After examining them to make sure I had chosen sturdy ones, she would braid the switches. That part of the ceremony was to establish her authority and delay the event.

When the moment of truth finally arrived, I would have to either wear short pants or roll my pants up so that she could get at my legs with the switches. As she delivered the punishment, I thought the unthinkable about Mama. Even today, I am afraid to repeat those words to myself.

The ritual was replete with unspoken psychological rules. You had to cry. But you couldn't cry too much or dance too much to protect your legs or you'd look like you were faking. You couldn't fake. If so, the ceremony would be prolonged. You could not look like you were being defiant either. "Boy, are you staring at me?" Mama would say if I got caught being defiant. "No, ma'am." You had to look her in the eyes and then break it off really quickly as an acknowledgment that you got the message of her authority status. Overall, the rhythm was choreographed and finely tuned to deliver love amidst the punishment.

The intent was not only punishment for wrongdoing but also psychological conditioning to survive in a racist society. Mama wanted me to understand that the purpose of the punishment was not to inflict pain but to build character. "This hurts me more than it does you," she always said during the Switch Dances. Although I swore up and down back then that the spanking did not hurt Mama any, I now realize that tough love is a difficult, and often painful, gift to give. My mama never abused me with punishment; rather she used it to teach me integrity and character.

Conversely, a psychologist with a liberal advocacy group at Columbia University promotes the belief in professional journals that spanking leads to negative behaviors such as aggression and delinquency. In the same unscientific breath, "she admits finding no causative evidence" that spanking is "mostly harmful."[24] In fact, even in her zealotry, she "could not think of a single situation when a spanking would ever be appropriate."[25] Being Black in America has historically been reason enough for Black parents.

To the nonsense that spanking should never be an option, White columnist Betsy Hart proves that common sense is not limited to Black parents as she intuits Mama: "If I told my kids all day long that I loved them like crazy, but never touched them, never hugged, kissed or held them, would they believe me? Of course not."[26] Right and wrong "sometimes needs a physical touch too"[27]—as a spanking appropriately given.

Unlike some middle-class parents today, Mama did not harbor guilt about adding corporal punishment to other more benign forms of control, such as removal of privileges, because she knew exactly why she was doing it. She knew she was raising a Black son in a hostile White world, and what that meant.

It would be easy for me to sit here today, and even easier for White parents whose children have never needed survival skills to cope in a racist world, and condemn this tradition as abusive treatment. But, in my opinion, that would be a mistake because you have to put this cultural phenomenon in the context of a racist environment in which, if you walked down the street and a White person told you to get off the sidewalk, you had better get off that sidewalk. Knowing how to appear compliant was an essential survival tactic. Mama loved me and taught me that, if I was going to make it, I had to know how to restrain my true feelings.

The world was changing, though. Every night on television, we watched young people beaten, children blown up, all in the name of safeguarding a racist system. We watched the dogs and the water hoses unleashed on our people in Birmingham. It overwhelmed Black America and all decent people throughout the world. It overwhelmed me to the point where I was no longer willing to contain my anger. In fact, I came near exploding with outrage.

In the 1960s and 1970s, all Aframericans had to make a choice. We had to choose whether we were going to commit ourselves to the destruction of everything White people stood for, or whether we were going to join the side that believed that the racist system could be destroyed without violence. Here, once again, the values Mama had instilled in me shaped my path. At this point, I was very angry with Whites—I want to be really clear about that—but I could not bring myself to hate them.

I never ever got to hate. The part of Mama that I carried inside would not allow that. When I felt like I wanted to hate White people, Mama would come up in my consciousness. She was always there. I always had that restraint that came from my upbringing: Hate is bad. It is morally wrong, no matter what the circumstances. I will defend myself, but I will not initiate violence. That is how, just by a hairsbreadth, I ended up in the Martin Luther King, Jr., camp.

But I also held the conviction that, in order for real change to happen, Aframericans themselves would have to change by rejecting the psychological dependence fostered by racism, and we would have to lead the changes in society. Charting our own course was not a finely worked out political philosophy, it was instinct. And, as I look back on it, I see that it was an instinct shaped by the examples of Black self-hatred that I had seen and experienced growing up.

I remember the moment when I first publicly articulated this conviction. I was in graduate school at Wayne State. I had already developed a reputation as an effective organizer, first of public events and then of protest marches. And I was always invited to the political gatherings that were held on campus almost every night.

We had a White Episcopal priest at Wayne State, Father Malcolm Boyd, who was very liberal and deeply involved with the students and our causes. People frequently gathered in his house for political discussions. One day I saw Father Boyd on campus, and he rushed over and said, "We are having a very important meeting about civil rights tonight. Please join us." I agreed and that evening went over to his place with a friend. We walked in, two Black guys standing in the middle of all these White people sitting on the floor. So we settled down, and by way of welcome Father Boyd says, "Tonight we're discussing the role of Whites in the civil rights struggle. What do you think?" The underlying assumption was that they should assume their traditional role of defining the Black movement and speaking for Black people, as one White man at the meeting later stated.

I was quiet for a moment, deciding whether I should say out loud what was on my mind. But my whole being was rebelling against the training in submission. I looked at Father Boyd and said, "I don't think you have a role in the civil rights struggle."

Everyone in the room was shocked. These were dyed-in-the-wool White liberals, solving the problems of the world from the safety of the university campus and away from the real Black world. They did not know anything about Black people or their actual struggles. Those of us they did know were in college, for the most part their socioeconomic counterparts.

"Black people have to assume responsibility for themselves and chart their own course. The task of redefining the Black community's sense of itself is ours," I continued. "This is our struggle, and we must be in charge of this struggle." Now that I had their attention, I could address their basic concern. White people had a role in the movement for Black equality, but no longer as liberal racists who infantilized Blacks and stifled our aspirations with habitual condescension. More Black people had to demonstrate more self-reliance to throw off the psychological shackles of slavery and segregation and, ultimately, empower themselves socially and economically in order to be equal.

From my intensity, the Whites in the room could sense this new reality, of a deeper and more profound purpose than the desegregation of public facilities, and realize for themselves that pity had run its course. I was saying that both Blacks and Whites should accept a new challenge. The challenge for Whites, I told them, was to transcend themselves so they could accept us as equal human beings. We would do the rest through the realization of our own worth and strength. I could not do their job for them, and they could not do mine. No one ever said that loving one another was going to be easy.

I was rebelling against America's status quo—not only against the racist system itself but even more passionately against the unconscious racial superiority of Whites and self-hatred of Blacks that the system had fostered. Now, looking back at it, many people will have a hard time believing that there was a time when Black people thought that White people had to lead the Black fight for equality, when both Blacks and Whites believed that Aframericans could not lead. The NAACP, however, was not the first civil rights organization. It was preceded by the Niagara Movement for Civil Rights, organized by W. E. B. Du Bois and a group of thirty Black professionals in 1905. "We refuse to allow the impression to remain that the Negro-American assents to inferiority, is submissive under oppression and apologetic before insults," the group declared.[28] But the Niagara Movement failed to generate popular support among Aframericans, and it folded in 1909, defeated by Black self-doubt.

After the infamous White-inspired 1908 race riot in Springfield, Illinois, which saw the destruction of the Black section of the city, a group of White liberals, largely Socialists and Communists, led by William English Walling, called for a movement to save Black people. That was the origin of the National Association for the Advancement of Colored People (NAACP). All the Black Establishment leaders wanted to be in this White-led movement; only Du Bois, as the public relations person, became an official and the NAACP's token Black. The Aframerican communities wholeheartedly supported the NAACP, mainly because Whites were in charge, and the organization succeeded.

That was the mentality we were all operating under at that time—in order for something to work, a White man had to be in charge. Even if we did choose a Black leader, he had to look like a White man. There was always a place at the table if you were a very light-skinned Black man, a Caucasian phenotype. We had a lot of confidence in you if you looked European, because we had been taught over centuries to put all of our confidence in White people.

That was where we were in our development at that time. In the biblical story of the exodus, the Jews whom Moses led out of Egypt took their slave mentality "into the wilderness" with them, and the self-hatred developed during their enslavement precipitated mistrust among them. But eventually they overcame and evolved from a tribe of former slaves into a great nation. So, perhaps, the contemporary African descendants of American slavery are gradually maturing.

Slavery and oppression had taught us never to initiate anything. It was literally beaten into generation after generation of Aframericans: You are completely dependent on White people. Do not trust yourself. And, God knows, do not trust other Black people. This was the dysfunctional baggage that Aframericans carried "into the wilderness" as a result of our experience during slavery and segregation. Black was not beautiful then, it was ugly. It was this dysfunctional self-hatred that I was rebelling against.

My experience, fortunately, was shaped by Mama—along with my sister Billie and Mrs. Norman and scores of other wonderful Black people who had raised me to be the person I am. I knew from them that it takes love to survive what we have survived. In the midst of my anger and outrage, I never doubted that it would be love that would lead us to equality. I was also convinced, however, that we had to start by learning to love ourselves.

"It's not what you call me, it's what I answer to," says the African (Yoruba) proverb. That is another way of saying what Mama had taught me about race: When you value your humanity, no one can strip you of it. Self-empowerment became the basis of my personal civil rights crusade. It remains my credo. I have discovered through decades of experience that when you believe you deserve health, wealth, and happiness, you create them.

Marching to Self-Empowerment

By 1963, I had begun to make a name for myself as a community activist through my writing for the *Detroit Courier* and my involvement in organizing performances, rallies, and marches. I used my column to mobilize people, to educate them about injustice and self-empowerment. I worked with my best buddy, Abraham Ulmer, Jr., who led a committee of the local NAACP branch to bring young people into the movement. I produced plays and dances to help the Aframerican community come together.

Shortly after Birmingham exploded in the spring of 1963, I got a call from James Del Rio, a Detroit entrepreneur whom I had met through my work with the *Courier* and who had become a mentor to me. "There are a few people getting together to talk about how we can help Martin Luther King in the South," he said. "I think this is something you should be in on." Del Rio was immensely successful (found as an infant abandoned in a garbage can, he was among the early crop of 1950s Black millionaires), and he had a lot of clout in the Aframerican community. I knew that, if he was involved, this was something big.

We met later in the week at the Urban League office. Ten or fifteen of the heavy hitters in the Detroit Black community were also there: Del Rio and Reverend C. L. Franklin, Aretha Franklin's father, who led one of the biggest Black churches in town and was himself a well-known gospel singer, and several other big-time preachers and businesspeople. I have to be honest, I felt very conspicuously out of place, because I was the only person there who did not have the kind of prominence they all had.

There I was feeling like the green youngster that I was among all these giants, and they were all saying, "We want to do something to help our people on the front line, but we don't know exactly what to do."

Aware that I was in the presence of my community's most respected elders, I very timidly said, "Why don't we have a march?"

"What kind of march?" somebody inquisitively shot back, encouraging my participation.

"Well," I reasoned, "we want to be free. Why don't we have a march and call it Walk to Freedom?" I could see people nodding, so I felt more confident and went on.

"Reverend Franklin," I said, "I understand that you know Martin Luther King personally. If we can get Dr. King to come and lead the march, we can call it Walk to Freedom with Martin Luther King."

"That sounds like a good idea," Reverend Franklin said. "Yes, I know Martin," he thought out loud. "I'll give him a call." (I had never heard anyone call Dr. King Martin. That was the sign that you were a real insider.)

The purpose was to raise money to help Dr. King's movement. There was this passion on the part of Northern Blacks to be involved. But what could we do so far away from Birmingham, from Selma, from the rest of the South? We could raise money to support the struggle. So the march was a way to get people energized, to rally them to contribute financially and morally. We figured we could get maybe ten thousand people to come to Cobo Hall, which holds twelve thousand people. We could get a dollar, maybe two dollars, apiece and raise between ten and twenty thousand dollars.

We formed an organization, the Detroit Council for Human Rights, to stage the event. I was appointed the coordinator of the march, and the rest of the group served as the controlling committee. We got a little office, and it and our volunteer staff were placed under my supervision. I worked around the clock for the next few weeks getting things organized.

I went door to door to all the Black institutions in Detroit, churches, clubs, Waymon Dunn's block club associations, you name it, asking whether they would send some people to the march. More important, I got the support of Chester Higgins, the editor of the *Detroit Courier*. He basically let me use the paper to promote the march. Leading up to the date, every week the headlines, front pages, inside pages, comics pages, society pages, sports pages said, "March . . . March . . . March." The surprising side effect was that the circulation of the little newspaper went way up, lifting my community standing with it.

And I learned the power of the mass media. I could tell from the enthusiastic response I was getting when I called on people that we had struck a chord. It seemed more and more clear that we would have not several thousand people but several hundred thousand. I still vividly remember a staging meeting we had with the Detroit police brass to lay out the route of the march, the feeder streets, security, and so forth. After we went through the initial formalities, one of the police representatives asked how many people we were anticipating. Everyone turned to me.

"Looks like two, maybe three hundred thousand," I said.

Well, everybody, especially the cops, almost fell off their chairs, laughing. "We've never had more than thirty thousand people show up for anything."

"You planning to get every Black person in Detroit into Cobo Hall?" someone asked, sparking another burst of laughter among the cops.

On June 23, the laughing stopped. From all over Michigan and nearby Ohio, between 250,000 and 500,000 Black people came out into the streets of Detroit to walk for freedom with Martin Luther King. This is attested to in a sworn affidavit of George Harge, retired deputy chief inspector of the Detroit Police Department, who in 1963 was a police lieutenant assigned to protect Dr. King during his stay in the city. This sworn document has been published by and is now in the possession of Judge James Del Rio. I am careful to document these numbers because skeptics tend not to want to believe that this sea of Black people assembled to demand freedom and equality.

I cannot think of another day in my life that comes close to that one. It was a transcendent experience for all of us. You could not have been there and not been touched, transformed.

I expected Martin Luther King to be full of life and vigor, to pose for the cameras, to glad-hand everyone. To tell the truth, I expected him to be as happy as I was. Instead, when I first saw him out in the street, I could clearly see his fear. He looked very worried, very solemn, stoical. (See the June 23, 1963, picture of Dr. King in Detroit at www.tonybrown.com.) Amid the waves and waves of people marching in support of the struggle he symbolized, Dr. King looked like the weight of the world was on him. I could not understand why he was not rejoicing at the sight of all these beautiful Black people standing up to racism. What did a man as famous as he was have to be afraid of?

Of course, that just shows you how naïve I was. I thought when you got to be famous, you got to be happy. I did not know that Dr. King's fame was exactly the thing that endangered him. Here was a man who was under the surveillance of the FBI and was battling its vicious smear campaign against him. There were daily threats on his life. He had been betrayed by many of his best friends, had been renounced by much of the Black leadership, and was feared by the Establishment. In short, he was a man who had sacrificed his peace of mind and had been marginalized for what he believed in.

In spite of his worries, though, he was very courteous, very polite. Everybody wanted a piece of him, and he tried to give a little bit of himself to each of us. He knew what he meant to us. It was a responsibility that he took very seriously. (You might say that he willingly died for all of us—as a humble "drum major for justice," as he called himself the night before he was assassinated.) But it was when he began his speech that his power really revealed itself. Every word of that speech was magnificent. And each of us in the overcrowded auditorium and the multitudes outside were uplifted and inflamed by the passion of Dr. King's dream, the dream of true freedom and equality.

It was a life-defining moment for me. I listened to Martin Luther King, Jr., and was inspired to bring a new meaning to my life by dedicating myself to helping Black people become self-empowered. My epiphany was the role I would play for the rest of my life. This was my Rosa Parks Moment. I wanted to eradicate every manifestation of racism and discrimination I could find, especially its psychological grip on Aframericans. I wanted Black people to learn to value their humanity, the way Mama had taught me to value mine.

After the march and meeting Dr. King, I went from being a part-time activist to being a full-time activist. I was not ethnocentric because deep down I believed that no one is superior to anyone else, and I rejected nationalism because it is too narrow and too selfish in its outlook. But I did believe that we had to have some showdowns and that people had to learn to see the world in a different way. I used my skills as an organizer and journalist to fight racial injustice.

I developed a stealth tactic that proved very effective against institutional opponents. As I tested my mettle, I went after the banks and the theater department at Wayne State University because they rationed Black participation. I organized pickets and wrote stories in the *Courier*. Within weeks, Blacks were taking part in the theater department's productions and workshops and working at every bank in Detroit. There were hundreds of injustices, large and small, that we tackled. Today, Wayne State University is the most desegregated institution of higher learning in the United States.

I wanted to do more for my community than break down barriers to White institutions, however. I wanted to help build our own social and human capital. I did not know how exactly I was going to do it or what role I would play in this process, but I knew that, by this point, I had enough skills and passion to make a difference. I quit my job as a psychiatric social worker and started my own company with three thousand dollars that I had saved. I rented a small office in James Del Rio's building and hung out my shingle, so to speak.

I will never forget the voice of the nice White woman at the telephone company who helped me get my first business number. "I am going into business," I proudly proclaimed, "and I would like my telephone turned on."

"Very well," she said. "What is the name of your company?"

I was stumped. "I don't have a name."

"Well, what is your name?" she asked.

"I'm Tony Brown," I said. "What do you think of Tony Brown Enterprises?"

"Oh," the lady said, "that sounds really good."

And I have been Tony Brown Enterprises, Inc., ever since. But back then, *enterprises* basically meant that I was going to do whatever I could think to do to lift up the Aframerican community. So the first thing I thought of was a magazine for Black people in Detroit. I called it *Detroit Set* (later *The Set*), with a nod to the famous *Jet* magazine. I put out this little magazine for a few months pretty much single-handedly. I sold the ads, I wrote the copy, the works—until Thad Foster joined me.

As I was learning about publishing, I was also learning about advertising. Often, when I tried to sell ads, the prospective clients would ask me if I could design the ads for them. So I started creating advertising. I quickly ran into a problem, though. There were no Black models. Here was another opportunity to make change, I figured. I went out and found Black people who were interested in acting and modeling, hired a photographer (Robby Roberson, with whom I covered Dr. King's most famous "I Have a Dream" speech, in Washington in August 1963), and Sandy Lawrence and Thad Foster started teaching people how to model.

Little by little, we became more sophisticated and came to be recognized as a company that effectively reached the Aframerican community. Pepsi-Cola Bottling Company of Michigan hired me to produce an annual stage production to motivate Black youth— "Come Alive." (Years later, Pepsi-Cola Company [PepsiCo] would sponsor *Tony Brown's Journal* on national television for over twenty years.)

Now we had Blacks and Whites coming to us who wanted the Black community to know about their businesses. In the process, we were inventing what is now called ethnic advertising and public relations. At that time, all we were focused on was helping Black people recognize their own potential and their economic and social power. From public relations, newspaper journalism, and publishing, it was only a short step to television. Everything I was doing was preparing me for what was shortly to become my life's work. But that is a story in itself, which I will tell in the next chapter.

I was not consciously aware of it, but I was putting Mama's teaching about race into practice with every step I took. My focus was exclusively Black at that time (it would take me many more years to learn fully Mama's lesson about race), but it was a focus on encouraging Aframericans to fight for health, wealth, and happiness by learning to value their humanity—a self-empowered freedom.

I continue to preach Mama's gospel. We are all God's children. Health, wealth, and happiness are our birthright. All you need do to claim them is honor your membership in the human race.

TONY BROWN

Wisdom

THE VALUE OF UNDERSTANDING HISTORY

"Today is the mother of tomorrow, Anthony," Mama would always tell me when she offered me the alternative to blaming others. "The world isn't fair, but if you work hard, you will get your share of success. And the world will change, too. It's changing all the time. Things are better now than they were when I was a girl. Our people have not gone into the promised land, but they will, because God's plan is that all of His children will be treated equally. Your job—everyone's job—is to work at being the best person you can be."

That was the wisdom Mama shared with me about the value of history: Each of us creates history through the actions we take every day. When we invest our energies in positive actions, we progress along the path to the health, wealth, and happiness that are our birthright.

It was that wisdom that I reached back for, as I always do, when I was asked to be the featured speaker at "Healing, Hope, and Reconciliation," the June 2, 2002, memorial service for the eighty-first anniversary of the Tulsa Riot of 1921. "My mama said, Never confuse knowledge and wisdom. Knowledge will tell you to hate someone because they've treated you wrong. Wisdom tells you everybody has to answer up sometime," I told the audience and the readers of the next day's *Tulsa World* in the five-column lead story on the front page by Randy Krehbiel, under the headline "Opportunity Lies in Adversity, Speaker Says."[1]

Mama told me that we humans would never be wise enough to judge one another, so let God do the judging. Relying on her wisdom, I told the audience that "the Tulsa Riot is now the Tulsa Opportunity." Rather than embrace another Hegelian cycle of conflict with Whites, Blacks can depend on the self-reliance of their ancestors to build a new reality. Inspired by Mama's words, which came through me, I went back to my hotel room that night and wrote a business plan (a market solution) to "Rebuild the Black Wall Street." (See Chapter 6 for details.) After over eighty years, it is time to rebuild with love. "Let's Do It Again" is my slogan and challenge to Blacks and Whites.

Another man who took Mama's advice and used her brand of wisdom at an extremely important juncture in history may have saved America from a lot more bloodshed on September 11, 2001. In the only interview that he gave after the terrorist attacks on New York and Washington, Imam W. Deen Mohammed, the spiritual leader of the predominately Aframerican Muslim American

Society (about half of the mainstream Sunni Muslims in the United States, not to be confused with the Nation of Islam), told me (on *Tony Brown's Journal*) that had Blacks followed the path of hatred, America and the world could have been a very different and much uglier place today.[2]

Imam Mohammed is not a new admirer of the idea of Americanism or the assimilation of Muslims into the American culture. The true significance of this long-standing commitment to his faith and American core values became quite obvious during the TV interview, considering the lucrative offer that he says was made to him five years before by a wealthy Saudi. He was offered a huge sum of money ($55 million, according to one source) to indoctrinate his Muslim community in the United States, I suspect, with an extremist, anti-Western worldview—much like the militant Wahhabism of Osama bin Laden that is so prominent among the al Qaeda foreign legion of extremist Islamists.

Little did America or its intelligence community realize that since 1993 hundreds of American Muslims had joined the foreign legion of America-hating terrorists. The goal of all extreme Islamists (often pretending to favor democracy and Americanism as a cover) is to install anti-Western theocracies that restrict rights for women and religious minorities. Terrorism is their chosen means to this end, similar to those means employed throughout history by Fascists and Communists. In Europe (and increasingly in the United States) a strident political Islam has been allowed to take hold in the segregated slums where illiterate imams call for an Islamic victory over Christianity and Judaism. A booklet printed in Saudi Arabia and distributed throughout Europe describes the aim of Muslim societies as "trying to become one day a majority through reciprocal assimilation with the non-Islamic majority which will gradually accept the morals and religion of Islam."[3] A number of prospective Arab terrorists and native-born Americans are being recruited for al Qaeda sleeper cells in Europe and the United States, where they have found a convenient haven, rather than in their home countries, where they are not allowed to openly teach such fanaticism. "Since 1993, Muslim extremists have recruited U.S. citizens—even those without Arab backgrounds—to their cause, reported the New York *Daily News*.[4] These jihadists are, to be sure, "a tiny minority of the nation's 4 million Muslims."[5] (Likewise, only a tiny minority of Christians who oppose abortion blow up abortion clinics.)

The Muslim community as a whole should not be blamed for acts committed by a few fanatics. Neither should the non-Muslim majority allow unassimilated Muslim ghettoes (Europe made that mistake) where fanatical imams indoctrinate their followers as violent Sunnis of bin Laden's Salafi sect, as was the case with American jihad Johnny Walker Lindh, or the al Qaeda warrior Abdul Hamid as he was known while fighting against Americans in Afghanistan. Fortunately (despite the comparativley few al Qaeda sleeper cells of U.S. citizens that are being uncovered), the overwhelming majority of Muslims—including many Wahhabis and 69 percent of American Muslims—who embrace Salafi teachings also reject the extremist fundamentalism of the Wahhabist/Salafist Taliban and al Qaeda's use of austere ideals of "political Islam" to justify acts of terror and suicide. It is safe to say that mainstream Islam rejects both terrorism and suicide.

Those Saudi-funded American mosques that spread Wahhabism (estimated at 20 percent or 250 mosques, and are, for the most part, resented by moderate Muslims who view "petro Islam" as a perversion of their faith) are under the influence of the Saudi Arabian sect of Wahhabism—or Salafism, as the broader, Pan Islamic movement is called. According to media reports, there is a consultative body of elite Wahhabis and Salafists in the United States that reports back to Saudi Arabia on the status of what moderates call "petro Islam" in the United States. Over the last forty years, the United States mosques that accepted the Wahhabi interpretation of Islam have been allegedly supported by billions of dollars of Saudi and other Gulf money.

Media sources have reported that these funds have allegedly been funneled through a Salafi-influenced entity in the United States to spread an often anti-American brand of fundalmentalist Wahhabism that ultimately seeks a world Islamic state: "When we are in power, there will be no more elections because God will be ruling." Intelligence officials believe that the "Brotherhood" mosques (where Aframericans and immigrants from the Middle East mixed easily) became a favored recruiting ground for al Qaeda's militant Islamist foreign legion.

Because he is one of "the most influential voices in Muslim America," as *The New York Times* identified Imam Mohammed, there is little doubt that, had a militant Islamist recruiter succeeded in bribing him to pervert the teachings of Islam, millions of U.S. citizens might have been religiously predisposed to attempt the destruction of their own country—a prospect so frightening that it is hard even to contemplate. Instead, Imam Mohammed continued to teach the nearly 2 million Aframerican followers in the Muslim American Society the traditional Sunni Islam shared by 90 percent of the world's Islamic faithful and the virtues of America. Because he may have single-handedly prevented a clash between his followers and the U.S. government when it was most vulnerable, a potential national catastrophe, I call Imam Mohammed a historic figure.

Mama taught me a long time ago that whatever I invest my energies in today is going to define my life tomorrow. Imam Mohammed told me that he refused to turn against his country because, as he has told his followers for decades, "America is one nation under God." All religions are respected in the United States and, therefore, the United States deserves the respect of all religions, Imam Mohammed told me. This is also his helpful advice to Muslims throughout the world.

America made an investment in Imam W. Deen Mohammed decades ago, and on September 11, 2001, it was paid back big-time by his love of the United States. America's love may have prevented a devastating religious-racial civil war. Unlike the biblical Lot's wife, Imam Mohammed kept focused on the future.

"It's best not to look back. Don't let your eyes stray from the path ahead of us that God has laid out, or He might turn you into a pillar of salt the way He did Lot's wife when she looked back," Mama jokingly taunted me with a bit of sly wisdom. However, she qualified her advice by saying that, while we look forward, we should always look inward.

Blaming White people for all of our troubles is like looking back—losing sight of the future. Looking back will cause Blacks to continue to live in a reality created by racists, in which they define us. Every ounce of energy we spend on blame is one less ounce available for creating our own reality that empowers us. We can either rebuild the Black Wall Street or some other symbol of past achievement or spend eternity complaining about what we don't have. Playing the victim is a losing proposition, because, as history teaches us, if you don't exercise the option of self-empowerment, someone else will control you.

Barbershop Puts "Noble Negro" Down

Controlling Black people's minds through censorship, in a classic example of misleadership, reared its ugly head in 2002 when a small-thought police squad rued unflattering characterizations of "sacred" civil rights icons in a movie. Jesse Jackson demanded that MGM re-edit and remove a sequence that he perceived as irreverent from its hit movie *Barbershop*.

Although Jackson never saw the movie, it was hard to find Blacks who (a) did not find it hilarious; (b) did not notice that the disparaging remarks about two civil rights heroes, Rosa Parks and Martin Luther King, Jr., were immediately refuted by other characters; and (c) did not wonder why these leaders paid less attention to important issues than to censoring a comedy because it was not a part of their political agenda. Still other Black people wondered why the outrage did not also include the prevailing sexist and racist sterotypes in the movie.

Let's face it, the truth value of this movie is quintessential Amos 'n Andy–type buffoonery, written, directed, and produced this time around by Blacks in Hollywood. Both Black and White audiences love it—just as Black and White audiences did decades ago in its original form. That's mainly why *Barbershop* debuted as the number one box office hit in the country. It laughed at Black leaders the way Whites laugh at White leaders and icons on *Saturday Night Live*. (During his time, the media said Abraham Lincoln looked like a monkey—as part of the rumor that he was Black.)

I don't object to *Barbershop* (it accurately depicts what goes on in Black barbershops) or to Black people laughing at themselves; that is very healthy. In fact, in this instance, it is good to see them laugh at their Black would-be censors. A cartoon from *The Philadelphia Daily News,* reprinted in *USA Today,* caught this undertow of distrust and resentment that many Blacks feel toward the misleadership of their so-called Black leaders. It showed two Black barbers behind empty chairs in "Jesse & Al's Barbershop" with a sign in the window that said THANK YOU FOR NOT JOKING, while scores of Black men outside were hiding from them.

Notwithstanding its commercial success and the fact that it was only an entertainment comedy that Aframericans adored and the right of Black filmmakers to enjoy the same freedom as their White counterparts, what I do object to is *Barbershop*'s conspicuous effort to marginalize the Black person who wants to be self-empowered. Somehow, he or she is not truly Black. In *Barbershop* this racist caricature of the self-hating, Uncle Tom jerk was called Jimmy, the only Aframerican barber who is college educated and articulate. That's how the traditional symbol of success and progress (what got us where we are) is degraded.

In an example of bizarre absurdity, life imitated art when an angry Harry Belafonte, the calypso singer, used the nefarious racial stereotype of Jimmy in *Barbershop* to liken Secretary of State Colin Powell, the first Black chief ambassador in history and the second most admired man in the United States, to an unprincipled plantation slave who would readily surrender his integrity to "come into the house of the master." Powell was, as usual, gracious in deflecting the racially charged comments from his "friend." However, Belafonte's strange and scathing outburst is belied by Powell's openness about being proud of his African heritage and his willingness to work and benefit groups inside the Black community. That is more than I can say about Belafonte's offspring, AWOL from anything Black, who has identified 100 percent with her mother's Caucasian heritage and deliberately stays far from the social reach of Black people.

Belafonte's demagogic use of a racial stereotype may be effective, since it has convinced many Blacks and Whites in the past that being Black and independent and successful are beyond Black abilities without prostituting your being. But Powell and millions of other Black people disprove this myth every day in a White world by succeeding on their own terms—with their integrity intact—because their focus is on reaching the height of human potential, rather than on bowing to fantasy stereotypes that promote vulgarity, ignorance, and failure. Both Powell and Belafonte are of Jamaican descent, and Powell, a huge fan of calypso music, has been known to tell associates that Belafonte's calypso-style performances are not genuine. That assessment certainly would match his latest performance as well. (Condoleezza Rice, the fiercely independent woman who manages the nation's security apparatus, bluntly exposed Belafonte's partisan plantation mentality when he racially savaged her: "I don't need Harry Belafonte to tell me what it means to be Black.")

Beside these racist Jimmy stereotypes at work in the character assassinations of Colin Powell and Condoleezza Rice and *Barbershop*'s Jimmy character, others saw what amounted to the movie's degradation of women being codified as part of the culture of Black men (on an individual basis, those views are in context because some Black men feel that way). Yet, a few prominent Black leaders had a selective hissy fit over one character's coarse lines in a two-minute sequence, which is fast becoming as famous as the shower scene in *Psycho*. The cantankerous Eddie character made the disparaging remarks that Rosa Parks "sure ain't special," although she started the Civil Rights movement—which renders his statement an oxymoron. (He's logically confused.)

Eddie's statement that Martin Luther King, Jr., was promiscuous, however, is debatable, albeit based in fact. Georgia Davis Powers, a former Kentucky state senator, wrote about her alleged relationship with MLK in a book (*I Shared the Dream*) and detailed it for me in an interview on television. There are other allegations of affairs also. Whether the movie's doggerel about King is true or not, it cannot discredit the work of this great man. The womanizing speculation certainly does not diminish my respect for Dr. King. As Ralph Abernathy, King's confidant and successor at SCLC, opined, the stress the men of the SCLC were under created weak moments, and the temptation to violate the biblical prohibition against extramarital sex overwhelmed many of them.

This entire exercise in judging King is ironic in the extreme because King made it possible for the Blacks who made this movie to get an education and a foot in the front door of the movie business. In fact, he sacrificially offered himself to death as a drum major of justice so Black fools could make fun of him in Amos 'n Andy movie remakes like *Barbershop,* and anyone else they chose, including Jesse Jackson who was crudely dissed in *Barbershop* as well. He was ordered with a four-letter word by Eddie, the curmudgeon in the movie, to go peform a sexual narcissistic act of contortion. Besides, the fact pattern established by Civil Rights movement figures about King's personal life has contained the same sexual rumors for the last thirty years. Why then did Jackson greet the brief risqué treatment in *Barbershop* with such moral outrage and hysteria, even demanding that the movie be re-edited? This casus belli against *Barbershop* backfired on Jackson among

Blacks like the woman who told a newspaper: "Jesse Jackson is not an icon or leader of the Black community. He's self-serving. He has his own ethical issues he has to deal with. He's open to criticism."[6]

Jackson himself has been challenged for over thirty years for maintaining that he, and not Ralph Abernathy, cradled a dying Martin Luther King in his arms, and later wore MLK's dying blood on his sweater to public meetings in Chicago. (See *America's David* by Barbara Reynolds.) Yet, for this and other indiscretions, he should not be held to a higher standard (a la "the noble Negro") than White House occupants such as FDR, JFK, or LBJ who could wink away extramarital affairs with a smile. I hazard to guess that if we purged history books of men and women who were linked to outside-of-the-tradition sex or marriages, there would be a lot of empty pages. All humans have faults, and if we want forgiveness, we must forgive others, Mama always told me. Jackson pleaded for forgiveness during his "Hymietown" crisis: "God's not finished with me yet." He's right, and that goes for the rest of us as well.

As a result of this cathartic movie, many Blacks began asking, "What's wrong with telling the truth?" Maybe these young Hollywood whippersnappers are teaching us that Blacks don't have to carry around the burden of "the noble Negro" stereotype (the one it seems Jackson and his Taliban committee on virtue are upholding) any longer. Seen through that prism, Eddie's irreverent remarks were liberating because the truth has no negative connotations (although it might hurt), Mama told me. Once again, and incontrovertibly, we are faced with the unavoidable truth: Blacks and Whites are basically the same. Most of us are average, but we have a few geniuses and a liberal sprinkling of fools.

A Foundation of History

Children never forget people who love them. I have not. The best way to describe the way Mama treated me is to say that she gave me honor. She honored me in the way she loved me. She honored me in the way she shaped my character. And she honored me with her example of a life lived well. In everything she did for me, Mama taught me that people who are confident, people who are responsible, people who chart their own course—in other words, people who are self-empowered—always have a destiny that is different from that of people who allow others to define them.

Power, of course, can come only from a sense of who you are. It is the value you see in yourself. Mama taught me that I have the power to create my own worth by setting goals for myself and succeeding. And she grounded that belief in the history of my family and my community.

Mama always wanted me to be proud of who I was, so she talked a lot about the history of the Browns. It was rumored in family circles, for instance, that the legendary West Virginia mountain man Daniel Boone may have been the father of William Wells Brown, America's first Black novelist and playwright, who was, in turn, the grandfather of my paternal grandfather, William Brown (who bore a strong resemblance to the famed writer). I am named after my grandfather. It appears that Daniel Boone, according to *The Atlantic,* "turned out to be descended from English royalty."[7]

I was interested in learning family history, but I was never inspired by the fact that some of my progenitors, even royal ones, were Caucasians who rejected and abandoned us because we also had an African ancestry. I am much more flattered by being the potential descendant of William Wells Brown, a Black man who gave the world wonderful words and beautiful ideas, than by possibly being related to an English king or queen from a group of Teutonic-German effete grandees who infected civilization with imperialism, racism, mercantilism, and colonialism.

In some cases, what Mama told me about my parents and their families was painful to hear, but she never withheld the truth from me. Instead, she helped me understand it and deal with it. Therapy that I highly recommend.

The Browns, as I said earlier, had a very high opinion of themselves and, in many ways, rightfully so, but not because they were partly White. They were Black octoroons, and saw themselves as part of the "aristocracy" of the Black South, people so light-skinned they were considered a separate race. They certainly saw themselves as separate from both Blacks and Whites, with a culture all their own. And they had privileges that other Black people did not have.

Grandpa Brown was a big shot in the state Republican Party. Most Blacks in his era were Republicans because Abraham Lincoln had freed the slaves and the Republican Party was founded in 1854 to stop the westward advance of slavery. As I wrote in *Black Lies, White Lies,*

Frederick Douglass and the first twelve Blacks to serve as U.S. Congressmen were Republicans. And Congressional White Republicans were the architects of Reconstruction, a ten-year period (1866–1877) of unprecedented political power for Black people. Democrats working hand in hand with the Ku Klux Klan gave us Jim Crow laws that effectively reenslaved Blacks. . . . Republicans spearheaded a movement to force Whites to give equal rights to the former slaves and initiated the Thirteenth Amendment, which outlawed slavery; the Fourteenth Amendment, which guaranteed Blacks citizenship; the Fifteenth Amendment, which extended the right to vote to former slaves; and the first Civil Rights Act of 1866.[8]

This was the tradition of the Republican Party of the nineteenth century, but, unfortunately, it is hardly the agenda of today's socially conservative Republicans.

Grandpa had an administrative job at the state capitol, and that was the height of success for a Black man in those days. He never recovered from the fact that Blacks, the poor Blacks first, broke with tradition and became more attracted to the Democrats because of the social programs of Franklin Roosevelt in the 1930s.[9] Read my first book, *Black Lies, White Lies,* for details on the history of Blacks and the two major political parties.

The Browns had a gorgeous home with an orchard in the back. It was like going to the movies for me, walking through that Shangri-la. It was beautiful, with orange trees and grape arbors everywhere. The house itself was also very impressive. The elegant living room, for example, was reserved for special occasions; otherwise everything in it was kept covered.

I remember the first time I was in that living room. One of my father's brothers, Sumner, lived in Chicago, where he studied classical music. He came home for a visit one day and performed a concert for the family. Dressed in a stylish tuxedo and wearing stage makeup, he tirelessly sang song after song. He was not a good singer, and all of us youngsters, with the exception of my older brother Nathan, who worshiped him, giggled incessantly through the long evening.

Like Uncle Sumner, the Browns were all very handsome people. As I said earlier, one of my aunts was a showgirl at the Cotton Club in Harlem, New York, where Black women could work only if they were light brown or near White in physical appearance, and where Black people were not admitted as customers.

So, the Browns, like all Black people, were forced into the peculiar institution of white supremacy and a world of color status. It was difficult to deal with, especially for me as a child, and the way it affected my siblings and me. Mama never wanted me to be ashamed of any part of myself, though, and she talked to me often about the accomplishments of the Browns. "You are a Brown," she would tell me, "and you have a lot to be proud of."

Mama also encouraged me to get to know my mother's family. The Pack and the Parker clans were very prominent in their own right, many in and around Hinton, West Virginia. Some of them were doctors and lawyers. I thought that my mother's mother, Mattie Pack Davis, the daughter of Mary Pack, half Aframerican and half Cherokee, was kind of odd. I did not understand that I was dealing with another culture, so she always seemed strange to me. She was very private and did things in her own distinctive way, not like other people I knew. She had an erect bearing, was very dark, and had black, silky hair, the same color as her skin. My exceptionally intelligent mother looked exactly like her; I considered both of them to be stunning in appearance.

Mama taught me about the history of our people as well, by telling me stories of her growing up and how things had changed since she was a girl. She did not dwell on how tough life had been, but told me enough to help me understand there was a generational opportunity I had that she didn't have. Mama never saw herself as a victim. And she did not want me to see her, myself, or any Black person as a victim. She wanted me to know that White people did not play fair, they had rigged the system, and that what we had to do was concentrate on outdoing them, on outperforming them, until the system became fair, as it surely would.

She would sit me down and tell me about a time when Blacks could not vote, a time when we were not citizens of the United States, a time when the Supreme Court decreed that each of us counted as only three-fifths of a human being. Mama also told me how during slavery Blacks were killed if we were caught reading. She told me of a time when we could not be educated, a time when we did not have beautiful schools with very well educated teachers, a time when there were no Black colleges. We could not work at the post office, could not be bus drivers, in fact, could do nothing but the most menial of jobs. Jobs in television would certainly have made her list of inaccessible options, but TV was too new on the scene. She made sure I understood that it had not been so long ago that there could not have been a Black person in the Olympics and that we could not have had a Joe Louis as the heavyweight champion of the world.

Mama held an unshakable belief that inequality for Blacks would come to an end. And she had a unique way of predicting a better future. Through her stories, she taught me that we had made progress, that this is a good country, and that the principles of Americanism would eventually help us win our full rights. Most important, she taught me that I had a responsibility to take advantage of the hard-won opportunities our people had struggled for, and not to let anyone, Black or White, deter my optimism.

This message was reinforced throughout the community in

Charleston. There was tremendous emphasis placed on being proud of Black people who had succeeded. In school especially, there was a lot of focus on what Black people had achieved, what we had to be proud of.

I went to Washington Elementary School, named not for George Washington, but for Booker T. Washington, who was born and raised about eight miles from Charleston. I attended Boyd Junior High School, named in honor of Henry Boyd, an inventor who bought his freedom and became a successful businessman. And I graduated from Garnet High School, named after Henry Highland Garnet, a descendant of the Mandingo warrior tribe in Africa and a militant Black leader who advocated a Black armed revolt in the mid-nineteenth century.

In "An Address to the Slaves of the United States of America," delivered on August 21, 1843, Garnet proclaimed: "Brethren, arise, arise! Strike for your lives and liberties. Now is the day and the hour. Let every slave throughout the land do this, and the days of slavery are numbered. You cannot be more oppressed than you have been—you cannot suffer greater cruelties than you have already. Rather die freemen than live to be slaves."[10]

We did not learn any of the revolutionary Garnet history as part of the official school curriculum, because that would not have been tolerated by the White Establishment, but we did bootleg enough Black history in school to have a sense of pride. Ours was a segregated school system. My buddy Scotty Calloway's father, the distinguished Andrew Calloway, was the superintendent of Negro schools. In effect, he was in charge of all of Kanawha County's "colored" schools—our elementary schools, junior highs, and high schools. All of our teachers and principals were Black. And between them, they figured out how to teach us about the achievements of Black people.

There was no Black history in the classroom, but every day during the homeroom period the teachers taught us about our people. The Black educators had developed a guerrilla curriculum that they used to supplement our lessons. So, we learned "his-story" in our official history classes, and we learned Black history through this unofficial system.

The standard curriculum taught the Western European version of American history, much of which is simply not true, especially when it comes to the oppression of dark-skinned people by Whites and the crucial link between Aframericans and the Nile Valley Civilization in Afro-Asiatic Egypt, Africa (Alkebu-Lan). Slavery was glossed over by this party line, which emphasized how privileged Blacks were to be in America. Fortunately, because we were being raised by a community that saw itself as separate but equal, we got not only the Establishment brainwashing but also the antidote.

Some of our schools also held Negro history celebrations. Negro History Week was started in 1926 by the Association for the Study of Negro Life and History and Dr. Carter G. Woodson, a great intellectual who busted the Talented Tenth (Niggerati) elitists in his classic work *The Miseducation of the Negro*. This was the precursor of Black History Month. During Negro History Week, each homeroom in my school would send its champion student to compete in the schoolwide Black history contest. Eventually, one student would be crowned the champion for the entire school.

The whole stealth system was set up to ensure that we learned to achieve and to take pride in who we were. We had institutions named for famous Black people. We had teachers who were professional, who dressed well, who took pride in being role models. Even the football coach had on a nice suit and tie every day. They assumed this responsibility to show us how to conduct ourselves, how to succeed.

From my teachers and from Mama, I learned to have confidence in myself, to know that I could compete with the best of them. I worked hard, because they had taught me that you shape history by investing in the future, and I succeeded.

In the seventh grade, I was chosen to participate in a statewide history contest. I was so proud to represent my school. I will never forget the day when our homeroom teacher ran into class all excited and announced, "Anthony Brown has won a Golden Horseshow Award." It seemed as if everyone in the whole school already knew and was cheering. I was on cloud nine. A short while later, I, as one of fifty-five county winners, was presented with an award by the governor in an official ceremony at the state capitol.

That was how our community equipped us to fight against the injustices of racism, by beating the system through superior preparation, hard work, a sense of pride, and some stealth education. We learned not to hate the people who oppressed us but to sublimate the negative energy that we would have used on hating them to loving ourselves and to use our achievements as a way to prove them wrong. The idea became second nature for me—using positive energy to solve problems.

The History of Self-Empowerment

This was the foundation of history that I took into adulthood and my work as a community activist. I wanted to use my voice to help Black people feel proud of themselves, to inspire them to invest in the future of their own equality. I guess I wanted the entire Black world to share Mama and Garnet and Charleston. I was beginning to get a real sense of the power of the mass media, and I could see that television was the way to reach the biggest possible audience. In addition, there were practically no Blacks on TV during this period, so I saw an opportunity to break down another barrier.

Well, my first attempt to get a program on television did not go the way I had planned it. This was in early 1967, several months before the "long hot summer," when America's urban areas exploded from Black anger. I made an appointment with the station manager of one of the local Detroit channels. I brought a mess of clippings, my magazines, a list of clients, and so on.

I introduced myself, told him about Tony Brown Enterprises, about my column in the *Detroit Courier*. "I am well known in the community," I said. "I've got a readership. And I would like to do a TV show."

His somewhat impatient but polite demeanor gave way to an expression that said in no uncertain terms that he had just been presented with the dumbest idea he had ever heard. And then he started to laugh—uncontrollably—literally holding his sides and fighting back the tears. "You want a television show?" he repeated, incredulous. "God, that's something. I've never heard anything like it."

But life is like a football, it takes some funny bounces. The very next day I was in the cafeteria at Wayne State, where I would occasionally drop in to have lunch. One of the regulars there was Sol Plotkin. He had been around the campus for years, one of these superbrilliant perennial-student types. Sol was a lawyer, but his real love was helping the underdogs. He was very political, very involved, very well connected, and had a real affinity for Black people. Sol respected Black people enough to offer his help or tell you to go to hell if you did not know a good thing when he offered it. He was a no-nonsense White liberal.

"Tony," Sol blurted out as he sat down at my table, "I had an idea this weekend. Detroit should have a Black person on TV."

"I agree," I said. "In fact, I was at a TV station yesterday, and the manager laughed in my face when I told him I wanted to do a show." Sol and I agreed to pursue the idea further.

In about two days, Sol called me at my office. "The communications students over at Wayne have ten thousand dollars," he said. "Someone gave it to them to produce a television series, and they have no idea what to do. If they don't come up with something really soon, they're going to have to give the money back. So I figured we could kill two birds with one stone. I told them about you, and I am pretty sure they will agree to give you the money to do a series."

A few days later, Sol and I met with the students, all of whom were White, and I told them my idea for the show. I wanted to do a four-part series: one segment on Black history, one on Black arts, one on Black entertainment, and one on Black politics.

They thought it was a fine idea. "Well, you'll need somebody to be the host and you need a producer," one of the students said.

At that time, I hardly knew what a producer did, but I figured that I had enough experience as a journalist to get the job done. "I will write the shows, and I will be the host," I said confidently.

"What about getting the guests?" someone else asked, sounding concerned.

I did not realize then that getting good guests is the trademark of a good producer. Will important people take your call? Success in television depends on who you can get to come on your show; that is how you drive the ratings.

"Oh," I said nonchalantly, "I can get anybody in the city. I know everybody."

We had in Detroit the crème de la crème of the Black community, people like Jon Lockhart, Carl Owens, and scores of other artists who have gone on to do spectacular things. Through my writing and involvement in the community, I knew all of the top Blacks in every field. I was certain that they would jump at the chance to be on TV, because it was near impossible for Blacks to get on television. So, I named a few people I thought I would be able to get for the show, and that sealed the deal. The students offered me the ten thousand dollars and their assistance to produce the series.

We worked for a couple of months, finished the four segments, and aired them on Detroit's public television station. Our timing could not have been better. In the midst of growing racial tensions and the unrest of the summer of 1967, we portrayed the life of the Black community in a way that had never been done before. The series may have been the first Black-oriented community television series in the country. The public reaction was a clear indication that there was a large potential audience for a show dedicated to Aframericans. And still, we could not get the funding necessary to keep the program on the air.

Everything changed, however, after Detroit—along with Atlanta, Boston, Buffalo, Milwaukee, Newark, New Haven, and New York—exploded during that summer. The violence of that summer was the worst expression of the racial tensions that had been building, and erupting, throughout the country during the 1960s. Urban rioting had become a regular feature of the national landscape, with inner cities rising up in 1965, 1966, and most intensely in 1967.

Following this stretch of riots, in which hundreds of people died, thousands were injured, and property damage soared into the millions, President Lyndon B. Johnson appointed a special commission to investigate the root causes of the rioting. The National Advisory Committee on Civic Disorders—better known as the Kerner Commission, for its chairman, then Illinois Governor Otto Kerner—issued its report in March 1968, concluding that the nation was "moving towards two societies, one black, one white, separate and unequal."

The commission laid the blame for the racial divide in America squarely on the White Establishment. "White institutions created it, white institutions maintain it, and white society condones it," the report said. "White society is deeply implicated in the ghetto," the report concluded.

The Kerner Commission investigation was the first serious look at race relations in this country, and its report was the federal government's first official acknowledgment of the fact that racism existed and was a serious problem. "The word *racism* had been used only by people who were deemed radicals," Roger Wilkins of George Mason University told CNN in a 1998 interview. "But all of a sudden here are corporate [chief executives], conservative civil rights leaders . . . [saying], 'If we don't mend our ways we are heading to two societies.'"[11]

It is significant that the Kerner Commission reserved some of its most pointed criticism for the media, concluding that the absence of Black journalists, and therefore a Black perspective, contributed substantially to racial inequality. The report went so far as to call for immediate desegregation of the media in employment and programming, which determines the images and messages the media project. The report stated, "Along with the country as a whole, the press has too long basked in a world, looking out of it, if at all, with white men's eyes and a white perspective. That is no longer good enough. The painful process of readjustment that is required of the American news media must begin now. They must make a reality of integration—in both their product and personnel."

This call to action had a surprising effect on my life. Shortly after the Kerner Commission Report (which became a bestseller, with over 2 million copies sold) came out, I received a call from the president of the Grosse Pointe chapter of the Junior League. I had only a murky idea of the Junior League as White ladies in white gloves and A-line dresses who held benefit luncheons for "the needy," so I was more than a little surprised when the woman who called told me that they wanted to discuss sponsoring a Black television show.

When Black people today try to engage me in playing the racial blame game, I always think about how I felt after that phone call. Here were these well off White women, most of whom were married to the power elite of Detroit, offering their support to a Black man to create a show for Aframericans. Instead of trying to maintain the status quo, they were using the resources of the Establishment to create change. They were out of the box—seeking freedom and reconnection, just as I was. You cannot come in contact with people like that and not be changed yourself. That afternoon in Detroit, I sat in my office and looked at the phone, thinking that Black people are not the only ones who should be judged, in Dr. King's words, not "by the color of their skin but by the content of their character."

Gil Maddox, who became the series' executive producer, and I met with the women from the Junior League a few days later, and they explained that they had undertaken a civic project to redress in Detroit some of the problems that the Kerner Commission had pointed out. Particularly, they wanted to help underwrite a television show for Aframericans, and they were looking for people with the talent and, they hoped, some experience in television and film. That meant the project needed Blacks with both creativity and know-how.

"We have seen the show that you did on public television, Mr. Brown," said the lady who seemed to be the spokesperson for the group, "and we think you are the right person to produce this series."

It turned out that the Junior League had obtained a grant from the U.S. Labor Department for this project. They also had gotten some wealthy Detroit residents to match it, and so had a sizable budget. In addition, they had lined up other resources, like access to camera equipment and editing rooms.

"We are very serious," they said to me. "We want to produce a program that will make a difference."

With the resources now available to me, I was able to learn all the nuances of television production, from budgeting through filming to editing. It was an exciting and productive time. I was working with the same kind of intensity as I had when I first started writing for the *Detroit Courier,* going nearly around the clock and still feeling energized and elated.

I named the series *CPT*. CPT, an initialism used among Blacks, stands for "Colored People's Time" because, we smile our understanding, we are habitually late. That was our way of telling Black viewers that the show was especially for them without ever saying it. On air, I would say, "This is Tony Brown for *CPT.* And, if you don't know what that means, stay tuned." But I never spelled out the title or gave an explanation.

My sponsors at the Junior League were very patient with my frequently needless militancy. Often, they did not know what to make of it. The truth is that all of us were learning to trust. There were times when they laughed nervously, but they never turned away from me. They were genuinely good people, people who reinforced for me Mama's value of history: They believed in building a better future by investing in the present.

These White women made it possible for me to gain a wealth of information and skills that would sustain my television and film career. I, in turn, used their resources and now my own to open the door for countless other Blacks who may never have gotten the opportunity to have a media career or the exposure. The Junior League itself is now multiethnic and is still involved in projects of this type.

Over and over in my life, in moments when I was about to lose faith and give up, people—Black and White—have come forward to remind me that to see the world the way we want it to be tomorrow, we must strive to create it today. There were always Black people and White people who challenged me to see humanity in terms of individuals rather than races.

The History of *Tony Brown's Journal*

In the 1960s, there were only two national television shows that targeted an Aframerican audience, *Soul!* and *Black Journal*. Both were produced by and aired on National Educational Television (NET), the forerunner of the Public Broadcasting Service (PBS). The highly popular *Soul!*, produced by Ellis Haizlip, was an entertainment format, and *Black Journal* covered the public-affairs beat. The mandate of the network was education, from instructional programs on. Most of the affiliates were college campus stations, and the network employed a segmented broadcasting approach. Segmented broadcasting introduced the idea of airing programs back-to-back that were targeted to different audiences. It was segmented broadcasting that made *Black Journal* possible in 1968.

William Greaves was the first Black executive producer of *Black Journal* (initially, a White man lasted for a couple of months), and he was the most prominent and respected Aframerican in television. In 1969, Bill got a grant to organize a conference of Black people working in TV and film—about fifty of us, excluding a handful in commercial TV who did not identify with Black causes and would never congregate with other Blacks. By that time, I had made myself a name in the television circles with *CPT* as a producer and on-air personality, and I was one of those fifty people invited to the conference.

We met in February 1970 at the Wingspread Conference Center in Racine, Wisconsin, and I recall deciding at the last minute to attend. I always joke that whenever two or more Blacks gather away from home, we form a national organization. Wingspread was no different; we founded the National Association of Black Media Producers. (When an organization is "National," it is usually Black; when it is "American," it is most often White.) I was honored to have been invited and to meet Bill Greaves, whom I admired very much for his cinema accomplishments and watched faithfully on *Black Journal* when it aired in Detroit. I participated enthusiastically in the discussions and, before I knew it, I was elected president of the new organization.

In keeping with my ideas on advocacy, I defined our mission as creating employment and programming opportunities in television for Aframericans. I threw myself into this cause. I researched the issues and discovered a legal tool to use in opening up the industry—the little-known Communications Act of 1934, which the Establishment had effectively hidden in plain sight. It authorized the Federal Communications Commission (FCC) to regulate the use of the nation's airwaves on behalf of its rightful owners, the people.

The role of the FCC, according to the authorizing legislation, is to protect the property of the citizens of the United States. The airwaves that broadcasters use to make money are owned by everyone in this country, the Communications Act of 1934 asserted. Therefore, according to the law, to earn the right to use the airwaves, broadcasters have to reflect the interests of the whole community.

Once I made this connection, I began to challenge the broadcast companies and local radio and television stations all over the country. Our argument was simple: The law says you must reflect the interests of every group in the community, and you have only White people working at your stations. You have no Black people in front of the camera. You have no Black people in management. You have no Black people in sales. In most places, they did not even have a Black janitor. The Black generation behind mine was not around during this era of overt discrimination and seems not to appreciate what it took to get them through the front door. They are all too eager not to identify with their own history. And that includes some Blacks who now own radio, television, and cable properties.

My anti-status-quo approach did not make me popular. In fact, it is one of the reasons that I have been rejected by commercial television. It did, however, produce the desired results. We did create jobs for a torrent of Blacks in TV and radio, and established a precedent in the industry. It was a new day, and the broadcast industry would never be the same.

By 1970, Bill Greaves, who was an independent filmmaker and had his own production company, decided that he wanted to leave *Black Journal* to return to making movies full-time. He came to me and said, "Look, put the word out that I want anybody who wants my job to apply. And I'd like to place your name on the list."

I said, "No thanks, Bill. I'm not interested. I've got my own business to take care of, and then there's the Association."

I was playing big shot, fighting for the cause. In the meantime, I was going broke spending my own money to run around the country creating jobs for everybody but myself. We had all pledged to put up a certain amount of money for the Association, but only Bill and one or two others paid their dues. So the work became a kind of personal crusade, but one I was not yet prepared to give up. That was why I told Bill that I did not want to be considered to succeed him at *Black Journal*.

"I'll tell you what, Tony," he said in his quietly insistent way. "There's very little chance that you'll get it anyway. You're number seventeen on a list of seventeen candidates. Don't worry about it."

Shortly afterward, I was in New York for business and dropped in to see Bill Greaves. We talked for a while, and then he said, "Let's step down the hall a minute. Bill Kobin wants to say hello to you." Bill Kobin was the vice president of programming for National Educational Television at the time, and one of the two men who were choosing Greaves's replacement.

We walked down to Kobin's office. He and the other top executive, Don Dixon, head of public affairs programming at NET, were there. They asked me how everything was going, and I was very happy to tell them how great things were, how we were challenging licenses and getting jobs for Blacks.

They listened to me, asked questions, and eventually we got

around to the best job in television for Blacks. Kobin said, "Well, listen, we've decided on somebody to take over from Bill." I was glad to hear that, because it meant that the most important Black TV series in the country would stay on the air.

At that point, Bill Greaves politely excused himself. Kobin paused until he left the room and said, "We want you for the job."

"Oh, no," I impulsively responded. "I'm doing something really important, and it's working well." I was adamant.

Kobin looked at me with these cool eyes and gave me his bottom line: "If you do not take over the unit, we're going to cancel the series. We need a strong person, a good leader. You say you want Blacks on TV. You say you want Black programming. You say you want Blacks to have jobs. Here is your opportunity. You will either take this job as executive producer of *Black Journal,* or we'll be forced to cancel the series, because we can't find anybody else who can produce and control the unit and make it productive. And we know you can do it."

What I did not realize at the time was that my priorities were out of order. When I look back at this moment, I cannot believe that I came that close to passing up the opportunity of a lifetime. Fortunately, I realized that, as important as the work that I was doing was, I could have a much greater impact as the executive producer of a national Black television show—the premier television series "for and about the Black community." And I would have complete editorial and budgetary control.

I did not want to be only the producer of the series, however, which was what Kobin and Dixon were offering. I had enough sense by then to understand that I did not want to spend my time branding a name that I did not own. I knew the value of a name. Besides, I love hosting, and I knew that I needed to be the host to translate the nuances of my mission and my vision, so I would not concede the point. The discussion was heated, and I almost lost. Fortunately, I was in a strong negotiating position, and I became the executive producer and host of *Black Journal*. By 1975, the series was so successful that Pepsi-Cola became our sponsor.

From the time I began, I had a mission for the series. I was convinced that if my largely female staff (the women didn't know it, but they were my tribute to Mama) and I could deliver the truth, we could educate enough people to create a critical mass that would set this country on the right course. So we set about uncovering and broadcasting the truth, as we understood it, which was radically different from the unapologetically racist TV genre of the day.

Over the years, we have had real breakthroughs. We were the first TV series to expose the Tuskegee Experiment, in which the U.S. government allowed Black men in Tuskegee, Alabama, to die from syphilis in order to study the disease. We brought the Tuskegee Airmen to the attention of the country. We were the first to make public the Tulsa Race Riot of 1921, in which a hateful White mob destroyed the famous Black Wall Street and the Greenwood business district. We were the first to cover modern-day slavery in the Sudan, and a list of firsts too numerous to name.

And here's a Black trivia quiz surprise: Denzel Washington, Academy Award–winning actor in both the supporting and leading actor categories, was a struggling Black actor when he made his national debut on *Tony Brown's Journal* (PBS) in "Malcolm and Elijah" in 1982. It was the first time he portrayed Malcolm X. Woodie King, Jr., who cast Washington in his two-man stage play, and I coproduced the television version.

In the process of pursuing stories, I have learned and discovered.

I have tried to present Black culture, Black politics, and Black thought in a variety of ways. And whatever we have done, I have always tried to give the historical background. I have taken what I learned in the homerooms of my schools in Charleston, West Virginia, and brought it to national television.

I have infused my work with Mama's value of history: I knew that if Black people were to succeed at being equal, we had to learn to invest in our future by honoring our past and shaping our present. I have attempted to help all Black people realize their worth—to demand respect, and to earn their equal rights to health, wealth, and happiness.

It has often been a bumpy journey. In the coming chapter, I will write more about the challenges I met in my pursuit of the truth and how this truth had transformed me over the years. Mama, however, has been proved right once again. The investments I have made throughout my life are paying dividends I could only dream of. I have gone all over this country and have met opinion leaders in every area of life who have told me that *Tony Brown's Journal* was an important influence in their lives.

"My mama made me watch you every week," many of them will say. Or, "I had to write papers for school about your show." I look at these accomplished people and think how blessed I am to see the future that I have helped create. All I have to do is watch TV or listen to the radio. And I silently thank Mama and all the people who have invested in me along the way.

History is made every day. Each of us individually, and all of us collectively, determine its course.

5

Truth

THE VALUE OF BEING TRUE TO YOURSELF

As I gathered my notes for this chapter, the country celebrated Martin Luther King Day. There was a slew of articles, tributes, debates about his positions on various issues, and analyses of his legacy. I was struck by the fact that, thirty-four years after his assassination, Dr. King still commands the power to capture the imagination of the nation, to inspire self-reflection, and to uplift our collective conscience. It is a power much greater than that of the leader, the symbol, the martyr. It is the power of truth.

"Truth, crushed to earth," Dr. King declared, "shall rise again." These words were prophetic, for the truth that he lived by lives on and continues to transform this country and the world.

I contemplated Dr. King's words and was again astounded by the similarities between what I learned from him and the values Mama had taught me when I was a boy.

"Anthony," Mama would say to me, "there's no keeping secrets from God." To a precocious child that sounded like an admonition to tell the truth. And indeed Mama placed a premium on honesty; the worst punishments I got were for lying. However, as I discovered over the years, what Mama was really teaching me was the value of integrity—of being true to oneself. "If you don't lie to yourself," Mama said, "there is no need to lie to anyone else."

And she taught me the value of this truth with every breath she took. Mama loved me as intensely as if I had come out of her body, but she never tried to be anything but Mama to me. She shared with me everything she knew of my biological family—even the ugly details—encouraged me to have relationships with my mother, grandparents, and siblings, and helped me decide how I would process all the information.

When we did not have enough to eat, when we did not have enough money, Mama explained why. She did not hide the truth from me; rather she made me a partner in making a plan to get some money. It is not easy for a parent to say to a hungry child, "We don't have enough today." But Mama's ego never got the best of her. She did not lie to herself, she was not ashamed of who she was, and she empowered me with her trust. I knew that Mama did not mislead me. If she told me that we did not have enough money to have chicken today but would have enough by Wednesday if we did this and that on Monday and Tuesday, I was sure we would be having chicken on Wednesday. In the process, Mama modeled self-reliance for me, rather than teaching me that Black people were perennial victims.

Implicitly, Mama taught me that you earn people's trust by being a person of integrity—a person whose actions live up to his or her words. She also taught me that trust is the foundation of a loving relationship. There cannot be real love where there is no trust. Therefore, to earn love, one must live with integrity.

This lesson went back to what Mama taught me about accepting yourself. She did not pretend to be anyone other than who she was, so she did not have to lie to herself or to others. Mrs. Norman put Mama's value of truth into words for me when she recited her favorite quotation from Shakespeare:

> *This above all: to thine own self be true,*
> *And it must follow, as the night the day,*
> *Thou canst not then be false to any man.*

It took me many years to understand fully the power of Mama's truth. And yet it is so intuitive. If you accept and love yourself for who you are, you do not have to expend energy trying to be someone you are not and you do not have to lie in order to convince yourself and others that you are this other person. All your energy can then be directed toward pursuing health, wealth, and happiness. This path, while simple, requires great courage. You have to be brave enough to tell yourself the truth about who you are, and brave enough to accept that not everyone is going to love the true you. The reward, however, is real freedom, the prerequisite of health, wealth, and happiness.

Discovering Truth

When I was growing up, Blacks were not allowed to swim in the municipal pool or the pool at the White YMCA. We swam in the river, at a spot behind the chemical factory that was called Nigger Beach.

South Charleston, West Virginia, the sister city of Charleston, is called the chemical center of the world to this day. And the area has a cancer rate that rivals that of the infamous cancer route in New Jersey to prove it. Of course, nobody has been able to "prove" that all the health problems that plague the people in that area are related to the chemical plants, but there is an obvious correlation.

Mama always told me to stay away from Nigger Beach because it was not healthy. "There are dead fish floating down there," she would say. "If you see dead fish, you should have enough sense to know it is not good for you."

Well, but Nigger Beach was where my buddies went, so I went too. There we were on a little strip of ugly beach strewn with broken bottles, swimming in polluted water with the chemical plant just on the other bank. That is where we went for fun.

We always did have fun, too, but somewhere in the back of my mind there was a sense of how unfair it was that the only place we could swim was this filthy, polluted "beach." This growing awareness was reinforced when Scotty Calloway's father, Mr. Andrew Calloway, who was the superintendent of colored schools for the county and who had a snazzy car, began to take Scotty, me, and two or three other buddies to swim in the pool at West Virginia State College, the local Black college, which was about a fifteen-minute drive outside of Charleston. It felt like such a wonderful luxury to swim and play in clean water. After that, every time I would pass the White YMCA in downtown Charleston and imagine I could smell that special scent of a pool, I would be filled with outrage at the injustice of the system that barred Blacks from the simple pleasure of swimming in clean water.

The opportunity to discover my truth about the injustice of segregation came to me unexpectedly, as such opportunities often do. When I was in tenth grade, Mrs. Norman asked me to represent the young people of our community at the dedication of the "colored" YMCA at a town-hall-style meeting. I was proud to have been selected for this honor, especially after I found out that I was scheduled to speak right before the keynote speaker.

I wanted to give a good speech, and I followed Mrs. Norman's advice to the letter. "Organize your thoughts into a succinct message," she had instructed. "Put them on three-by-five cards, use psychological triggers, read the ideas over and over, practice in the mirror, project your voice, use your diaphragm, and remember, we love you and we want you to do well."

I wrote the text and enlisted my sister Billie to coach me on my delivery. Billie was as tough as Mrs. Norman and as caring as Mama and, by now, my surrogate mother. I practiced, refined, and practiced more. By the time of the event, I was nervous but ready to face the large crowd. In my mind's eye I could see myself delivering the kind of stirring address that the famed Paul Robeson had given from the same podium I would be using.

When I came to the podium and faced the capacity crowd in the Garnet High School auditorium, something unforeseen happened. I could have sworn that I smelled the moist scent of the White YMCA pool. I hesitated a moment, a lump in my throat, a tightness in my chest. I thought it was nerves, but then I put down the stack of three-by-five cards and began to speak spontaneously, to voice the truth that was in my heart.

"Why have we come tonight to celebrate a damp, raggedy old building with hand-me-down, smelly furniture and flat-sided Ping-Pong balls and pool tables that run downhill?" I demanded to know in a voice that had a new note of power in it. "Why are we pleased with a facility—if you can call it that—lacking even a swimming pool, while the White YMCA has a first-rate pool just two short blocks down Capitol Street? Why are we content to be second-class citizens and to celebrate our second-class role tonight? No, thank you. When we have something to celebrate, let's do it. Until then, let's do what we have to do to have equal facilities and equal respect under the law. Thank you and God bless you."

I half expected the roof to fall in on me. There seemed to be a momentary silence, then the creaking of seats as people got to their feet, and then a sustained and enthusiastic ovation—the biggest one of the evening. I looked over at Mrs. Norman and was relieved to see her beaming approval at me. I felt reborn. The truth had set me free, and it had won me the respect and admiration of my community. I felt as if Mama had been there and had helped me find the voice of my people.

A couple of days later, however, I learned my next lesson about truth. As it turned out, the keynote speaker at the dedication ceremony was the chairman of the board of the White YMCA. After my performance, he made some brief, polite remarks, acknowledging the truth in what I had said, and went back to his seat. Although I had upstaged him, he seemed to be genuinely moved by my remarks, and he asked me to deliver the exact same speech to his colleagues on the board. I agreed, seeing an opportunity to make a real difference. I was not naïve enough to expect a standing ovation, but I did expect at least some nods of tacit approval. Instead, I was met with a hard, disapproving silence. These men wanted no part of me or my truth. To them, I was nothing more than an uppity "boy," whom they would soon run out of town, along with scores of other young Blacks.

This experience brought home to me Mama's teaching about integrity. Truth felt like oxygen. When I spoke what was in my heart, my whole being breathed with strength and vigor. Even when my truth was met with hatred, I found courage and power in the knowledge that I was being true to myself. From that point on, I saw my mission in life as a quest for truth.

Truth in the Trenches

I entered public life with the conviction that racism would not end until Aframericans overcame its legacy of self-hatred. I wanted every Black person in America to experience a Rosa Parks Epiphany, to believe that they deserve five-fifths of the joy and dignity of being a human being.

That was my life's mission, the mission I brought to *Black Journal* in 1970. In the program brochure for the 1971–72 season, I laid out the show's philosophy like this:

My Brothers and Sisters, *Black Journal* is produced by Black people to Black people for the liberation of Black people. It is a tool in the struggle for dignity and pride in ourselves.

So much of what *Black Journal* has come to mean to the

Black community is expressed in this excerpt from a poem by an inmate in a state prison:

> *A swelling that comes up from within*
> *A knotting in the chest . . .*
> *The glorious feeling of complete*
> *UNITY AND BROTHERHOOD*
> *And a sincere sense of being*
> *LOVE*
> *WE, the society's so-called*
> *Socially rejected, have a NATION*
> *And once a week it has become*
> *OUR DUTY*
> *To watch BLACK JOURNAL*

The traditional use of mass communications in this country has been for the purpose of oppressing non-Whites and entertaining Whites. The result of this vicious misuse of communications has been a general disrespect and misunderstanding by Whites about Blacks and Blacks about themselves.

If a White man could understand what it is never to have seen an image of oneself portrayed with dignity on television or on film, never to have seen an image of oneself portrayed in the simplest of human terms—love, marriage, birth, death—then perhaps he would have some comprehension of the "knotting" in the chest.

"YES, Black is beautiful. YES, Black is strong. YES, Black is intelligent." This is the message that BLACK JOURNAL carries to the Black community, a message mutilated almost to the destruction point by the broadcast industry—one of the most lily-white institutions in American society from the standpoint of control, management, and content of the material it puts before the public.

White producers who have played at being soulful, have indulged in either ridicule or absurdity, degrading us with programs such as the bigoted *All in the Family* or fantasizing our problems with shows like *Julia*. Other White producers have simply ignored us.

In this wasteland stands BLACK JOURNAL. BLACK JOURNAL reflects the Black experience honestly, reports on Black news, investigates and discusses Black problems, and promotes Black pride and dignity. It does this primarily by practicing "Black Journalism."

Black Journalism in its search for the truth, which may frequently run counter to White journalism, is a belief in the beauty, the power, and soul of Black people. It is a morally legitimate and tactically sound revolt of the oppressed against an oppressor. It reports on a community psychically in a state of revolution—a revolution against the tyranny of caste and color, not the political or economic order, but a revolution, nevertheless. It is a revolution as an act of hope and a revolution which prefers truth to war, which does not seek to destroy but to reform America.

Credibility? The standard of accuracy, completeness, objectivity, balance, and fairness is an ideal that no thinking person would dare challenge, understanding that we imply a White frame of reference. But since each of our respective social and psychological milieu has developed its own special brand of honesty, can an absolute be developed to measure an abstract? Superimpose the effects of White racism on both Blacks and Whites and subsequently one race's ability to understand the other's aspirations looms as a formidable task.

For too long Black people have been subjected to exhortations of Whites who in the name of "objectivity" have imposed their subjective views on the world about us. There is another witness with important evidence—the Black man with a Black viewpoint. And only through the airing of a Black perspective will the former slavemaster, who invented racism in the first place, begin to approach an honest understanding between the races. But as long as there are those who, in their own racism, intentional or unintentional, are quick to label a point of view which does not agree with their own with such epithets as "communist propaganda," we are still a long way from that small beginning.

From Guyana to Mississippi, BLACK JOURNAL shows its viewers how Black people are living and what they are thinking. Problems such as housing, busing, representation, and education are reported from a Black perspective by Black experts. . . . In addition, BLACK JOURNAL furnishes a platform on which serious Black spokesmen can expound their views—a platform heretofore denied them through institutional racism (currently most "talk shows" have boycotted those Blacks with a philosophy relevant to the Black revolution). . . .

Even though BLACK JOURNAL is by Blacks and about Blacks, its strong pro-Black stance does not necessarily mean that it is anti-White. Black pride and anti-

Whiteness are antithetical. Black pride is positive and productive. Anti-Whiteness is a negation of Black dignity
which, regardless of what form it takes, focuses on the
strength of the White man while overlooking the strength
and power of the Black man. . . .

Black people have spent most of their lives fighting the
struggle of self-hate that every institution in America
teaches. By promoting Black pride through the use of
Black Journalism, and providing a platform for Black
views, BLACK JOURNAL is and will continue to be an
antidote to this psychological self destruction. As one
viewer observed, "BLACK JOURNAL is our medicine."

As you might imagine, and as I expected, this philosophy was
not embraced by the Establishment. Co-option replaced exclusion
as the strategy for silencing Black voices. I got my first taste of this
new strategy shortly after I took over as the producer and host of
Black Journal. John J. O'Connor, who was then the television writer
at *The New York Times,* invited me to lunch. "What are your plans
for the series?" he said after we had exchanged pleasantries and
ordered our food. "What is your orientation going to be?"

As the producer of a show that was shaping Black public opinion
during a time when race relations were of paramount importance
in this country, I was asked that question practically every day.
"Well, the idea here is to help Black people understand their history," I replied, "to give Black people an opportunity to see themselves depicted from a Black point of view."

"But there is so much White people don't know about Black
people," O'Connor said incredulously. "Don't you think that as the
only Black person in America with a national television series that

is dealing in public affairs you have a responsibility to help the races understand one another?"

"Look, Mr. O'Connor," I said, "I don't think that the biggest problem Black people have is that White people don't understand us. Our problem is that as a result of several hundred years of racial hatred we have learned to hate our own race. And I intend to do everything I can to help Black people recover their sense of pride so that we can empower ourselves, not wait for someone else to understand us."

"What about the poverty, the social problems that have resulted from segregation?" he said in a controlled voice that was betrayed only by the rising color in his face. "How do you hope to address those if you don't educate the broader public about them?"

"What would you have me do," I said, also getting heated, "go to Harlem every week and report on how bad off Black people are? What do I achieve doing that? I just exacerbate the miseries of the Black community; the Black people watching are more depressed than they were before the show. White people cannot do for Black people what Black people refuse to do for themselves.

"No. If I am going to go to Harlem, I might report that there are more rats in Harlem than there are in White areas of the city, but that is going to be 1 or 2 percent of the show. The other 98 percent is going to be about somebody in Harlem who is doing something about these rats and then using that person as a role model, so Black people all over America can do something about their rats. I want people to say, 'Mrs. Jones did it in Harlem. I can do it in Chicago. I can do it in Mobile. I can do it in Los Angeles.' That's what the mission of the show is, to get Black people to say 'I can do it.'"

My tone made it clear that my rhetoric and I were the same. Mr. O'Connor was intellectually outraged but outwardly calm. He gave me *the* look, and very little of any consequence was said as we finished our lunch. From that point on, however, I was his enemy.

In a review published shortly after our meeting, O'Connor wrote: *"Black Journal,* a production of the NET division of the Educational Broadcasting Corporation, is controlled by Black people, is about Black people and, clearly, is for Black people. The White viewer can certainly tune in, but he cannot expect any accommodation to his particular point of view." In other words, he was almost flatly saying that White viewers should not bother watching the show. Although he did concede, in a backhanded way, that there was something White people could learn from the series: "He [the White viewer] may be puzzled or startled at times, but he may also learn something about race relations in the United States, something beyond what he might find on, say, *The David Frost Show* or the *The Flip Wilson Show."*

Implicit in O'Connor's words was the label of *radical* that would follow me from those early days of *Black Journal.* And I am radical: I am committed to a serious uprooting of the status quo. I was trained by Mama to change the world, and I have lived my life by that truth.

Truth, however, has to be defended, as I have learned many times over. After he realized that I would not carry water for the Establishment, O'Connor seemed determined to use his considerable influence to discredit me and *Black Journal.* His reporting became increasingly strident in its criticism, ultimately culminating on December 28, 1971, with a demand that public television drop my series. As a pretext, O'Connor used a segment of the show during which Dr. John Henrik Clarke, the renowned Black historian, cast the Roman Catholic Church in an unfavorable light. That alone, the outraged O'Connor (a Roman Catholic) suggested, was grounds for eliminating the only show on television that spoke directly to Black people about the issues that affected their lives.

I responded with a press conference (and covered by a writer from *The New York Times*) to defend myself. I will be eternally grateful to genius-man Ossie Davis and brilliant-woman Ruby Dee for standing up for me and my right to be my own man—to live by my truth. I was really defending Dr. Clarke's right to present a version of history different from the Establishment "norm," something that at the time was taboo everywhere else on television.

Thirty years later, Dr. Clarke was heralded as one of the unsung heroes of Black history by the *New York Post:* "His destiny was set in high school, when he read an essay called 'The Negro Digs Up His Past' by Arthur Schomburg. It was here he realized that African people in America had a history, and he set out on a mission to find it. . . . This world-renowned teacher served at the Africana Studies and Research Center at Cornell University in Ithaca, New York, and the African and Puerto Rican Studies Center at Hunter College, where he was Professor Emeritus of African World History. . . . This master griot's [oral tribal historian's] life and work have made him an integral part of the history he loved, studied, and taught so well."[1]

Mama's lessons about truth allowed me to withstand the attacks that I came under as a result of my commitment to provide a forum for the voices of the courageous pioneers, such as Dr. Clarke, who were redefining the meaning of Blackness in this country.

Truth shielded *Tony Brown's Journal* against attacks by White—and a few Black—journalists who were hired to protect the interests of the Establishment media. There were, of course, exceptional White and Black reporters who told it like it was. "Year after year, *Tony Brown's Journal* continues to fight the good fight," Michael

Cottman wrote in *New York Newsday*. Cottman proved that someone understood: "Over the years *Tony Brown's Journal* has become a media watchdog for news and information, not only for the Black community, but for the nation as a whole. Adding a unique insight to in-depth reporting, Tony Brown has established himself as one of the country's leading journalists and at the same time built a loyal following of informed Americans. . . . Tony Brown seems always to give you the unique side of an issue that the traditional press either overlooks entirely or woke up to months later."[2]

"Every negro is a potential Black man and every Black man is a former negro," I wrote at the time in the program brochure. "Blacks will not survive unless negroes are recruited fast enough. We *must* recruit negroes to the struggle. At this stage they control the skills, influence, and affluence, but they do not possess a sense of worth or understanding of who they are. . . . But that's our job as conscious Black people, to liberate our kind from their self-deprecating concept of themselves. . . . We must not insult them . . . or harm them in any way. We need them too desperately and love them too much to do that."

Empowerment Television

In August 2002, I became the chief executive officer of Urban America Television Network (UATV). I will continue to do at UATV what I have been doing for over thirty years as the head of my own television and film production company and the executive producer and host of *Tony Brown's Journal* (which continues on PBS).

A few months after becoming chief executive of UATV, I was

inducted into the prestigious Silver Circle by the National Academy of Television Arts and Sciences. I felt very honored to join such icons of professional television as Walter Cronkite in the Silver Circle and because the Academy felt that I had "made enduring contributions to the vitality of the television industry, and set standards of achievement for all to emulate." I was especially thankful for the "standards" acknowledgment of my body of work and life commitment—because if anyone emulates what I have done, they will have to emulate truth and empowerment.

At this stage of my career/life, programming television shows to empower people and to praise Black culture and heritage is almost an instinct. As I have throughout my life, I remain at odds philosophically with anyone who does not believe in the potential of Aframericans. Put in historical context, UATV is simply my latest self-reliance crusade to help build wealth (and sometimes income) in every home that participates in our televised empowerment programming.

I very much acknowledge the value of synergy between viewers and broadcasters (the secret of PBS's success). Throughout my broadcast career, I have maintained that television needs to balance its legitimate business and programming interests with the real-life needs of the consumers, our viewing audiences, especially a mostly Aframerican audience, with its unique history and the problems that resulted from that history. Since 1619, Aframericans have been intentionally miseducated by institutional racism and undereducated largely as a result of racism-induced poverty. The prescription for this predicament is reeducation and economic self-reliance. Therefore, the primary goal of a Black television network should be to help as many people as possible become middle class. And to do that, the broadcaster must focus on useful information and helping people empower themselves through more wealth—unity, income, and education.

If commercial television can be used to make money for advertisers and broadcast owners, it can also be used to help members of the community who buy the advertisers' products earn an income. Black people, 12 percent of the United States population, are a very generous and powerful market, with a gross domestic product of almost $700 billion ($900 billion in 2007). Broadcasters realize that fact and "major advertisers are just beginning to learn that Blacks are increasingly affluent, are brand loyal, spend more on disposable goods than Whites and watch 40 percent more television."[3] In a market system, generosity of that magnitude must be rewarded—not taken for granted. The Black community is a unique psychographic and demographic market, and it needs special consideration and VIP treatment by both advertisers and broadcasters.

This view of the world and television programming is fundamentally different from that of the executives of Black Entertainment Television (BET), the country's largest Black-oriented TV network. BET has refused consistently to recognize community empowerment as a business asset. Its critics believe that BET's viewers are perceived as mere entries in the ledger. Morley Safer said on 60 Minutes, BET "is making a fortune exclusively off Black America."[4] Blacks who watch BET are not stupid, but a starving man or woman will eat anything. 60 Minutes also reported that despite "low ratings," BET earns "high profits"—as only a monopoly can.

A squandered opportunity is the way Black cartoonist Aaron McGruder characterizes BET. "When you're in a position to change people's lives through positive representations, and you choose not to because you've taken the lazy way out with cheap shows that pander to sex and violence and money, it's just inexcusable. . . . You have a network that reaches 55 million homes and you're beaming in informericals about blenders and exercise machines."[5]

BET admitted in a filing with the Securities and Exchange Commission that its programming for Black people is weak and it is vulnerable to a television competitor that would target a "full service network" at Black Americans.[6] Safer stated, "Johnson's [BET's CEO's] critics within the Black community accuse him of pandering to the basest taste—junk sex, junk violence, nasty and nastier rap."[7]

Johnson justifies BET playing music videos (supplied by the record companies) 60 percent of the time because BET's (1999) audience of six million Black households is not big enough to demand the advertising rates that could raise enough money to produce quality programs.[8] But, as *The Washington Post* points out, Spanish-language networks that reach audiences of the same size and "niche" cable networks create their own programs. The truth is that BET, with $200 million in annual earnings, refuses to invest in its audience. "His (Johnson's) gospel is black dollars should go into black pockets—his pockets," *60 Minutes* reported.[9]

Johnson would have us believe that all of BET's critics are self-serving malcontents. "Why do they pick on BET? Why not ABC or NBC or FOX?" Johnson wonders. Black people feel betrayed, and with very good reason. They built BET's $200 million-a-year empire that was sold at a very handsome profit to Viacom. ABC, NBC, and FOX are not Black institutions, and they do not carry "Black" as a business designation. BET does. These White-owned media have no familial obligation to the Black community, and they were not built on the back of Black money and loyalty. BET was.

The White media did not make Robert Johnson America's first Black billionaire. Black people did. BET has used the disadvantaged condition of our community to make money, unlike the White networks. The problem between BET and the Black community has nothing to do with the White media. The problem is that BET owes Black people and it refuses to pay them—even to acknowledge the debt.

A very profitable BET that truly cared about Black people and demonstrated this sensitivity in its programming could have led the way to an even more profitable company and paved the way for the Black community's self-empowerment decades ago. Had BET shared a vision of empowerment for the Black community, it could have been a true pioneer in helping build a new reality for Aframericans.

As CEO of UATV, I hope to capitalize on the opportunity to empower the Black community that BET chose to pass up. I will rely on my vision of self-reliance as a foundation for creating empowerment programming and generating long-term advertising growth. A community where the people have been systemically oppressed for centuries needs something unique, other than mainstream escapism. We will offer programming intended to empower, educate, and entertain members of the Aframerican audience. For example, the series that I host on UATV is called *Empower the People.* It focuses on market solutions to social problems and empowerment through entrepreneurship. The other programs run the gamut from cooking to sports to Caribbean culture.

Succinctly, Urban America Television Network (UATV) can be

described as a new, creative, and unique, perhaps revolutionary, use of television as a media tool to help empower the people. Not only will UATV's signature programming be empowering, but it will be as culturally diverse as the nation and the world itself.

UATV is market conscious, but color blind because the only color of freedom is green. That's why we are "urban" (culturally diverse) in our marketing approach, which is based on the facts and the potential of business success. The Aframerican community of 36.7 million alone, located largely in urban areas, has a GDP equal to the eleventh richest nation in the world.

For over thirty years on national television, I have demonstrated leadership and an expertise in the cultural and economic aspirations of this viable sector of our economy. In some measure, I have been instrumental in helping the business sector (especially Pepsi-Cola, my corporate sponsor for over twenty years) understand how to communicate and benefit from a viable relationship with Aframericans. Put in historical context, UATV is simply my latest self-reliance crusade to help build wealth (and sometimes income) in every home that participates in our televised empowerment programming.

Therefore, UATV's primary goal will be to help as many people as possible became middle class. And to do that, UATV will focus on useful information (as well as entertainment and culture) and helping people empower themselves through more wealth—unity, income, and education. It is more than apparent that if commercial television can be used to make money for advertisers and broadcast owners, it can also be used to help members of the community who buy the advertisers' products earn an income.

UATV recognizes the fact that we must first earn the respect— via programming that enhances the culture and history of its viewers—and also create income-producing programming opportunities for the viewers as well. In less than two years, UATV's distribution system has garnered enough affiliates in the United States to deliver 20 million viewers via Telstar 7 satellite (www.urban-america-tv.com). Our cable affiliate in Miami alone has 700,000 homes and 2 million potential viewers. Furthermore, since the new economy is global, so is UATV. Our main affiliate in Europe is BEN Television, a culturally diverse channel with "a guaranteed reach of 6 million digital homes in Britain alone" (www. bentv.com). Millions more in twenty-two countries across Western Europe tune in to BEN via the Eurobird satellite, which also covers parts of North Africa (Morocco and Algiers). BEN's potential European audience is 70 million and will become a reality as these viewers add receiving dishes for the Eurobird satellite.

Our global approach also includes over 150 potential affiliates in the Caribbean. We are already in St. Croix, St. Thomas, and parts of Puerto Rico. David Simon, executive vice president of operations of UATV and formerly president and owner of Sun Television, is an expert on the Caribbean region and its music and culture.

In less than two years, UATV can conservatively estimate its potential total global audience at well over 100 million with the inclusion of the BEN network and the Caribbean. BET, after over twenty years, has 71.9 million potential viewers, according to *Fortune*.[10] I think you might agree that the Urban America Television Network is off to a very good start.

The Power of Truth

Advocating for institutional change, as I had done back in Charleston when I spoke at the dedication of the "colored" YMCA, has always been an essential aspect of my fight against racism in this country. From my early days as a community organizer in Detroit, and throughout my career, I have worked to end systemic discrimination.

I have always believed that the media played a special role in the struggle for equality. "Until we defeat the racism in television," I wrote in 1971, "which determines the fundamental concepts of seeing ourselves through white-eyes, and as W. E. B. Du Bois calls it 'a double consciousness' which teaches us to hate our Blackselves, we will remain slaves to our own enforced oppression. Until we make television reflect *our* reality, *liberation will remain rhetoric.*"

As president of the National Association of Black Media Producers, I mounted challenges to the licenses of many radio and television stations around the country, with the help of various local Black community organizations, such as BEST (Black Efforts for Soul in Television), headed by Bill Wright out of Washington, D.C., and Jim McCullough, executive director of Action for a Better Community in Rochester, New York, with a lot of help from David Honig, now a brilliant communications lawyer. Our goal was to use the Federal Communications Act of 1934 to open up the broadcast industry to Blacks.

In 1971, I became the first Black to address the National Association of Broadcasters at their annual meeting in Chicago. I took the opportunity to remind them that the 1934 law gave all citizens, including Blacks, the right to be on television and to work in the industry. After my speech, an infuriated White television executive from a commercial network stormed toward me. He was literally shaking with anger and his face was beet red as he told me that he had just placed a call to New York and that I would be fired the moment I returned to work. "If we are forced to hire all of the Blacks in America," he concluded, "you'll be the last one to get a job."

What this man did not understand was the power of truth. The NET executives, Don Dixon and Bill Kobin, for whom I worked were not interested in perpetuating racism. Don and Bill were as passionately committed to Mama's value of truth as I was. And today, over thirty-one years later, I own the company that owns the longest-running series on the PBS network, and I am still its host. That is the direct result of the tremendous support I have had from the Black community and righteous, fair-minded people of all ethnic backgrounds.

My commitment to fighting for equality and justice won me the designation of "television's civil rights crusader" from *Black Enterprise* magazine in a September 1979 cover story. And my efforts off-screen were as important as *Tony Brown's Journal* in advancing the agenda of bringing racial equality to American airwaves.

In 1971, as the host of *Black Journal* and the president of the National Association of Black Media Producers, I was one of the most highly visible Black people in the broadcast industry. That year, the president of Howard University approached me and asked if I would help them find a dean for a new school of communications, which they had been planning for four years but had had trouble getting off the ground. I agreed and drew up a list of about fifteen or twenty people who I thought would be good for the job.

"We have looked at all those people," the president said to me a few weeks later, "and we feel that you would be the best qualified."

"Me?" I said, feeling that this was déjà vu all over again, the same conversation I had had with the executives at NET about the *Black Journal* job. "But I am happy doing what I am doing."

"Well, couldn't we work out a deal where you could do it part-time?" the president asked.

It was an exciting opportunity to help shape the next generation of Black media professionals, so I said, "Sure. Let's see if we can work it out."

I talked to my bosses at NET, and they gave me permission to take three days a week and set up the School of Communications at Howard. So three days a week, every week for four years, I woke up in New York or somewhere else as the producer of *Black Journal* and I went to Washington to be the dean of the School of Communications at Howard University. Or I woke up in Washington and went to New York or somewhere else. Regardless of the direction I was traveling, I had to catch a plane practically every morning. Fortunately, the salary I received from Howard, $37,000, covered my travel expenses, because, honestly, I would have done the job for nothing.

When Howard University does something, it attracts a lot of attention in the Black community. And this was particularly significant, because even if we were not the first communications school at a historically Black college, ours was the largest and most sophisticated. We had a lot of money and a lot of brains and talent involved. We also got a lot of attention from the media. Educating Black people and training them to be better citizens was something even the Establishment press of those days could get behind.

At Howard, I was extremely fortunate to have Larry Still as my associate dean and Benjamin Cooke, who initially worked for me, as a professor in the speech department. Cooke later became the go-to guy in the School of Communications and, together with Still, one of the most loyal and truest friends I've ever had.

My idea for Howard's School of Communications was to make it more than a place for classroom instruction. I wanted it to be a testing ground for some of the ideas about the media proposed by the Kerner Commission Report. We had an opportunity, as I saw it, to train Black people in the precepts of independent journalism—a journalism of freedom—in the context of media outlets that were controlled by a Black institution. I chose "A Search for the Truth" as our motto and Frederick Douglass ("Power concedes nothing without a demand"), a Black journalist and abolitionist, as the school's symbol.

So, in addition to recruiting staff and a faculty, developing a curriculum, and setting up a course schedule, we launched a radio and a television station. The radio station, under the direction of Phil Watson, went to the top of the charts almost from day one. We had these brilliant young Black students speaking to a whole generation that had never been addressed by their peers through the media. Suddenly we were number one in the ratings. Howard University's radio station is still a major player in the Washington, D.C., market. The TV station was also very successful; it is now one of the premier stations in the PBS network.

My vision for the school went even further. I wanted it to become a key institution for changing the American media landscape. In order to accomplish this, I organized an employment conference. Traditionally when a university or college holds such a conference, it is for their students only. We opened up our conference to all comers in order to create opportunities for everyone in the Black community who was professionally qualified.

We identified two groups of participants: potential employers and potential employees. I went around the country and recruited any Black person who was qualified. We put a special emphasis on this point, because that was our selling proposition to potential employers. "You say you cannot find Black people to hire," I told news organizations, public relations firms, government agencies. "I am going to solve that problem for you. You come to this conference, and I guarantee you will have hundreds and hundreds of qualified people to choose from."

And we did. There were only a handful of Blacks who had jobs in communications at that time, but they all came. Everybody who was trained and qualified was at that conference. It was a dream come true for corporate America. Here was a pool of highly qualified Black people, and all they had to do was show up. In order to attend, however, the companies had to be serious. I told all the potential employers: "You cannot come to this conference and use it as a public relations gimmick, having your picture taken with a Black person. If you do not hire somebody, you will not be invited back next year."

The first conference we held was in February 1972, and we got 80 jobs. The following year, we got 150. The next year, we got 400. The growth was exponential, and today many of those people are in top positions all over the world, as executives in major news organizations, magazine editors, TV and film producers, etc.

For this and similar activities, I gained the media reputation of having the very valuable knack of interpreting Aframerican interests and relating these interests in media advancement to certain enlightened interests of the media establishment community in a way that is "positive, constructive, and creative," as one man once put it, rather than simply negatively reactive.

My truth is that Black people are capable of great accomplishments given a fair opportunity and that equality and justice benefit all Americans, regardless of race. Every success I have had in my life flows out of that truth. The Howard University School of Communications, which flourishes today as one of the best communications schools in the country, is part of my legacy of truth, a legacy that began with Mama.

Nothing Succeeds Like Truth

Mama taught me that being true to yourself, living with integrity, was the greatest success to which a person could aspire. I did not doubt her sincerity, but I was also tempted by the promise of worldly fame and fortune. Money has never been the most important thing in life for me, but I have always considered it an essential element of self-empowerment.

That is why I say that money is not the most important thing in life, but I rate it right up there with oxygen. It has taken me decades to learn the difference between money and wealth. Once I did, I saw the wisdom in Mama's teaching: Integrity is a keystone of wealth-creation. Not all rich people are wealthy. Some rich people have low self-esteem because they are not sure if people like them or their money. Out of confusion and the lack of confidence, they fail to build wealth.

Cathy Hughes always comes to my mind as an outstanding example of building wealth through integrity. Cathy and I met when I was dean of the School of Communications at Howard. She was living with her baby son, Alfred Liggins, in Omaha, Nebraska, at the time, struggling to make ends meet. One of my department chairmen who had worked with Cathy in Omaha recommended her. When we met, I saw potential in Cathy and hired her as an assistant.

Cathy helped put together our first communications employment conference and did an outstanding job. She subsequently was put in charge of radio sales, then the university's radio station, where I chaired the oversight committee. Cathy is now the rich chair and founder of Radio One, a $280 million (the rough equivalent of actor Tom Cruise's fortune) company that owns sixty-five radio stations, and the first Black woman to head a publicly traded company.[11] But more important than being rich, Cathy is also wealthy. It is part of a family tradition that goes back to her grandfather, Laurence C. Jones, who founded the Piney Woods Country Life School in Mississippi in 1909. Today, it is one of six boarding schools left for Black youngsters.

Cathy's personal legacy started off with one little station in Washington, D.C., which she got out of bankruptcy. She made WOL a part of the Black community. She and her son lived in the back of the station, and Cathy knew everyone in the neighborhood. She was not there just to make money off the people, she was there to build the community.

If people had trouble getting their Social Security checks, Cathy would go down to the government office with them and help straighten things out. If there was a landlord who was harassing tenants, she would be there to give them advice on how to protect their rights. Cathy was empowering herself and her community, and she used her radio station to do it. In so doing, she took that one little station out of bankruptcy and built it into an empire. She did it by staying true to herself and creating social and human wealth, individually and collectively, rather than just making money.

Cathy's success is a shining example of Mama's value of truth. (Corporate executives and Wall Street learned that lesson in 2002 when the "infectious greed" bubble burst.) Integrity, indeed, is the foundation of health, wealth, and happiness. There can be no greater success than serving others by being true to who you are.

"Do well while doing good," Dr. H. Naylor Fitzhugh, my mentor, instructed me, as Mama had done. And I have followed that success formula throughout my career. At times, I have been frustrated by what I saw as my failures to inspire the Aframerican community with my message of self-empowerment. As I will tell you in the next chapter, these perceived setbacks helped me understand and master Mama's value of patience.

$\mathcal{P}atience$

THE VALUE OF "KEEPING THE FAITH"

"Glory also in tribulation," Condoleezza Rice, the first Aframerican and woman national security advisor, paraphrased from Romans 5 in an interview with *Essence* magazine, "because tribulation breeds perseverance and perseverance patience, and with patience comes hope. And hope is never disappointed, because of faith in the glory of God."[1]

As I read these lines, the "self-contained woman in an Armani suit" in a corner office at the White House dissolved in my mind's eye, and in her place I saw Mama knitting at our kitchen table in Charleston. That passage from Romans 5 sums up everything Mama taught me about the value of patience—the gateway to health, wealth, and happiness.

Mama was the most hopeful person I have ever known. She had optimism that drew its strength from her faith. In a dark room, Mama could always see the light. And her faith gave her the patience to see beyond the trials and tribulations of the moment.

"There will be a day, Anthony," Mama would always tell me, "when you will have heroes other than Joe Louis." She knew in her heart that God's plan was equality and justice for all His or Her children, and she tried to instill in me the patience and hope she derived from that faith.

I have to be honest with you here, patience is not one of the virtues I was born with. From the time I was very young, I have always wanted to know and do things beyond my years. I was not an easy child to raise. I was very active and smart, meaning I could think up dumb things to do. I was always trying to figure out what things were about, how things were made, and so on. If Mama said not to go to the other side of the street, I would assume that there was something over there I needed to learn and would cross the street. That was how my mind worked. I was really a handful, but whatever scheme I came up with, I could never outsmart Mama.

"Sonny Boy," she would say to me, "take the time to grow up, you'll be a better man for it. You'll get everything life's got in store for you, when the time comes. There's no rushing God."

More often than not, I got frustrated with her, too precocious to heed her lessons on patience. But what Mama could not teach me in words, she showed me by example.

One particular instance of how patient Mama was with me has stayed with me all these years; I come back to it over and over to draw on her teaching about the value of patience. From the time I was old enough to remember until she passed on, I always accompanied Mama to church on Sundays. One Sunday—I must have been about eight—I put up a particular fuss about going. Mama did not make too much of it and let me stay home.

The tradition was to cook Sunday dinner before going off to church, so we could eat right after we came back. This Sunday, Mama fried up a big plate of chicken—my favorite to this day, although I now eat it rarely. She placed a nice white napkin over it and left it on the kitchen table.

"You be good, Anthony," Mama said while kissing me good-bye. "Stay in the house. We are going to have our dinner as soon as Mabel and I are back from services."

Well, the smell of that chicken was too much for me. As soon as Mama was out of sight, I decided to steal one piece. I liked the leg, so I took one and ate it. I then carefully rearranged the rest of the chicken on the plate to hide that a piece was missing. But I was still hungry, so I ate a second piece. And then another and another. I just could not stop eating that chicken. I was like a drug addict who constantly has to have the next fix; every time I ate a piece of chicken, I needed another. I kept eating until, to my great surprise, I had eaten all of the chicken.

It was obvious, even to a precocious eight-year-old, that there was no way to hide the fact that I had eaten the whole chicken. When Mama got home, I was prepared to take my lumps. I did not even wait for her to ask me what had happened to the chicken.

"Mama," I rushed to tell her, "I was hungry, and I ate the chicken."

"Oh, Anthony, you must have been very hungry," Mama said, unable to hold back a smile. "That was a big chicken."

I was expecting her to be angry or disappointed, since I knew I had done the wrong thing. But she just kept looking at me with that funny, sly expression. She did not come out and laugh, but I sensed that she got a secret delight out of the fact that I had eaten the entire chicken.

I think Mama could see my confusion, because finally she drew me to her and said, "It's wrong not to think of other people, Sonny Boy, but I know what it is to be hungry." She hugged me a little tighter, and nothing more was said.

Consideration of other people was at the core of Mama's lesson in right and wrong. Too bad some of America's college professors couldn't have stopped by one day for some of her delicious fried chicken and a homespun lesson on ethics. One poll found that 73 percent of college students said they were taught by their professors that uniform standards of right and wrong do not exist, that what you do in life is morally relative, depending on your point of view. Mama knew better, because she knew the truth. She knew that it was wrong for me to have eaten the entire chicken, since it left the rest of my family with nothing to eat. An action that benefits one person at the expense of the greater good cannot be right. Mama's lesson was that I would have benefited more had I thought of my family first and shared the food. That's a truth with which even the morally challenged cannot argue.

That Sunday I learned a lesson about the value of patience that I have carried with me my whole life. Sure enough, Mama showed me how to have faith in people in the face of their imperfection— and my own. When I am tempted by frustration, I think back to that empty plate under a white napkin and remind myself that I also "know what it is to be hungry." And sometimes the hunger is not for food but for simple acts of kindness.

Patience—faith in humanity—is the soil in which hope flourishes. And hope is the wellspring of health, wealth, and happiness.

Learning Patience

Mama planted the seeds of patience in me, but it has taken decades for me to learn its true value. My whole life has been about creating change, making things better, first for the Aframerican community and subsequently for all of the human family. As a young man beginning my career as a community organizer and civil rights advocate, I took to heart the words of Martin Luther King, Jr., about "the fierce urgency of now." In the electrifying "I Have a Dream" speech he delivered in Detroit and then in Washington, Dr. King sounded a call to immediate action: "This is no time to engage in the luxury of cooling off or to take the tranquilizing drug of gradualism. Now is the time to make real the promises of democracy; now is the time to rise from the dark and desolate valley of segregation to the sunlit path of racial justice; now is the time to lift our nation from the quicksand of racial injustice to the solid rock of brotherhood; now is the time to make justice a reality for all of God's children."

In my youthful zeal, I assumed that all Aframericans were equally impatient for change and passionate about creating a true democracy. I believed that, because Blacks had suffered for centuries at the hands of Whites, we were somehow more spiritually endowed, even superior to Whites in our sensitivity to other humans. If we could only free ourselves from the economic and educational restrictions imposed on us by the racist society, we would demonstrate a true humanism, of which American Whites, because of their history as oppressors, were incapable.

If only, I believed, we could produce enough professionals. If enough Blacks, for example, could gain access to medical schools, we would come back to aid Black people—unlike the White doctors, who are greedy and selfish—and improve health and life expectancy. We would return from law schools with much-needed legal expertise to defend poor Blacks in an America where you can get only as much justice as you can afford. And we would become leaders of the government but would reject the cup of political corruption and avarice so endemic to America's political institutions. We would never steal from the despised and dispossessed who sacrificed so much to put us in office and faithfully delegated their constitutional authority to our trust.

I believed that to topple institutional racism we had to have some showdowns. We did, and a lot of people, including me, learned their lessons. One of the first sobering experiences I had during that time was watching Black people who sat out the marches and boycotts insert themselves into the negotiations with the Establishment institutions that were being forced to open their doors to Aframericans. They took none of the risks and reaped most of the benefits, often at the expense of the greater good.

I made peace with the fact that there are demagogues who are part of any movement for social change and that the civil rights era was no exception. What eased the pain of that disappointment was that those of us who were intimately involved in the Civil Rights movement had a pact—a silent, tacit agreement—that if we made this country better for ourselves, we would not forget the rest of our people. We knew that if we went up against racism and succeeded in changing the system, it was almost inevitable that we would become part of the new system. We were often the best educated, the best qualified, and if the barriers fell, we would be the first to benefit. The pact demanded that we use the system to help educate the uneducated, to get people off welfare, to eliminate quotas and open up colleges and professional opportunities. We would use whatever power we accumulated to make life better for those without power.

As time passed, social change came and Black activism won the day. We won our freedom and the opportunity to be doctors, lawyers, and politicians. We are now admitted to law schools and the bar in larger numbers than ever; and we charge poor Blacks three hundred dollars an hour—just like White lawyers charge poor White people. We now graduate from medical schools and play golf on Wednesdays and avoid practicing medicine among the poor during the rest of the workweek—just like White doctors. We have gained access to the halls of power—and the political trough. And now that we are just as close to the cashbox as Whites, Black politicians steal at the same rate that White politicians do.

I watched all these changes come to pass with great joy, but also with frustration and disappointment. I watched some Black leaders and their cronies become shakedown artists, pretending to defend the Black community from White people while doing close to nothing to help the community lift itself up but everything possible to build dynasties for their offspring. The pact that we had made seemed to go by the wayside as self-interest took hold.

My disappointment found expression in a maxim I coined: Black people and White people are basically the same. Most of us are average, but we have a few geniuses and a liberal sprinkling of fools.

Once the tinge of bitterness wore off, however, these experiences brought me to a new level of understanding and compassion. Mama had told me all along that there was no difference between Black people and White people. I could not see it because the only people I saw in power were White people. I never saw anybody

Black in power, therefore I never knew how Blacks were going to act when they got in power until I became an adult. And then I saw what Mama was talking about.

Mama knew more about human nature than most people. Her wisdom came from her faith. She knew that God never did choose anybody: He or She never made anybody better or worse than anybody else. A person who is greedy is not greedy because he is Black or White. A person who is generous is not generous because she is rich or poor. And each of us behaves in a way that has been shaped by our experiences.

This recognition of our universal humanity brought me closer to understanding and embracing Mama's value of patience. It became easier for me to see people's actions not only in political and racial terms but in human terms. And with that, it became easier to accept them for who they are, because I was no longer afraid to identify myself beyond being Black.

Patience and Self-Empowerment

As I moved away from seeing everything in Black and White, I became more and more convinced that we were all enslaved by the brainwashing of the authoritarian Establishment. The Hegelian dialectic of race is designed to keep the effete ruling classes in power by separating human beings from one another and our own power.

America has enslaved itself in materialism. We have more than enough money but very little common sense. Just look at the adverse impact of twenty years of personal greed on the stock market and the nation's economy. Amid material plenty, we are suffering and starving spiritually. As Bob Marley put it: "In the abundance of water, the fool is thirsty."

The bottom line is that, if we do not change ourselves, we cannot change our reality. If you want something different, you have got to become a different person. Blaming someone else for our problems does not work. We cannot blame the bad people of the world for our problems. You and I—the people of goodwill—are responsible. The bad people are not responsible. The bad people are doing their job: They are creating fear and chaos.

You see, there is only one reason that Black America is in the shape it is in, and that is Black America. There is only one reason White America is in the shape it is in—White America. And the only solution, ultimately, is to empower ourselves to change.

You saw Rosa Parks inspire a new reality and change of consciousness for Blacks on December 1, 1955. Aframericans have not created a new reality consciousness since. Instead, the Middle Passage Fixation and attachment to a permanent victim status threaten to marginalize many Blacks in an America where a variety of ethnic groups are amassing growing economic and political power.

Self-empowerment, as I said earlier, has always been the mission of my life's work. In the early days of *Tony Brown's Journal,* I focused a lot of attention on helping Black people learn their history so they would understand how much we had to be proud of. I believed that if we had faith in our heritage and if we understood history, there could be no Black person who would not seize the opportunity to be the best.

As the barriers of institutional racism fell, Aframericans made tremendous strides. Yet, as a community, we still bore the scars of oppression. All too easily, we succumbed to the role of victims in the face of White supremacy, believing that we had no control over our own destiny.

As a Black person who had grown up with segregation, I understood that this reluctance to accept the fact that we are in charge of our lives was the result of the hundreds of years of brutal racial oppression. I was frustrated by our failures, but I understood them.

However, I still wanted Black people to be the best we could be. I made it a point to present—on the television program, on the radio, in writing, and in speeches—empirical evidence that we are capable of competing, that we are capable of better intellectual achievement, that we are capable of organizing our communities better, that we are capable of creating more wealth, that we are even capable of trusting one another. I also explored the residual effects of institutional racism that create among Blacks distrust of one another, which I saw as our greatest problem.

Increasingly, I saw the belief that the world owes us something—fueled by a Black leadership almost fixated on dependency—as one of the greatest obstacles to the maturation of the Aframerican community. "I don't know what White people owe us," I began to say in my speeches. "But I know one thing: They are not going to pay us." My message was that the only way to get ahead in this world was to understand that there is nothing wrong with getting knocked down, but there is something really wrong with not trying to get up. "The ground is no place for a champion," said Muhammad Ali.

The way I saw it, Black misleaders were taking Aframericans down the road of being permanent victims. I just wanted to pull my hair out when I heard them say things like: "We can't make it. You are doing well only because you are an Uncle Tom. Only Uncle Toms can succeed." In other words, failure is Black and success is White.

They were creating a reality for themselves that no thinking person, Black or White, wants to be in, a reality in which all achievers are sellouts, all good students are failures, all top earners and producers are traitors. Once you define the world that way, you are left with nothing but the angry, the failures, and those who will never amount to anything. And then you pass that legacy along as being Black. That sounded like a foreign language to me. I just could not go along with that because it was contrary to everything Mama taught me and everything I had experienced.

At this time, my reputation as a radical changed to one of, as one friend put it, "an equal opportunity ass-kicker." I must admit that I was, and still am, much more frustrated by Black self-hatred than I am by White attempts at supremacy. White supremacy I understand in an abstract way, as some White people's need to feel superior to someone in the face of their own lack of self-worth. Black and White racists share that same insecurity. It is much harder for me to understand why Black people would ever think of surrendering freely the opportunities we fought so hard to win.

I say, take the word *should* out of your vocabulary. The point is what you are going to do about the problems that you have, not how you are going to try to arrange this system so someone else takes care of them. Whether they should take care of things or not, whether someone else is responsible, whether someone else has treated you badly, all are legitimate issues. But they are not germane to your eating today or to your raising your children today. They are things to discuss, things to work on, but the top priority has got to be building up our community, one person at a time— now. Even if it is unfair, it defines reality, because life is unfair.

My Black brothers and sisters, we need to talk. I am just going to say it straight. We always talk about wanting a different outcome. But do we work to create a different outcome? Do we challenge ourselves to think for a different reality?

Black America does not get it. Aframericans spending $645.9 billion a year (after taxes) represent 12 percent of the American population, but we buy approximately 18 percent of the orange juice sold in the United States; 20 percent of the rice; 21 percent of the scotch whiskey; 26 percent of Cadillacs; and 96 percent of Florsheim shoes. Black women, 6 percent of the U.S. population, consume over 36 percent of all beauty and hair products. Black teens buy over 50 percent of all CDs purchased. Blacks between the ages of twelve and twenty-four purchase over 50 percent of all tickets sold in movie theaters. My numbers may be dated, but they make the point about the power Blacks wield. If you took Blacks out of the American economy, Wall Street would collapse "last week," I like to say.

As a business, UATV has identified the nation's most lucrative niche market: Urban America. Broadcasters have begun to realize the fact that the urban market is literally a "Black Gold Mine." And major advertisers are (not too far behind) just beginning to learn that Blacks are increasingly affluent, are brand loyal, spend more on disposable goods than Whites, and watch 40 percent more television.

Think Black for consumers who demonstrate the dominant buying power for goods and services such as telephone services, personal care products, electricity and natural gas, children's apparel, footwear, alcoholic beverages, automobiles, medication, travel, groceries, furniture, and men's and boys' apparel, to mention a few.

Black America is the eleventh richest nation in the world. And yet, what is the first thing that comes out of everybody's mouth when they describe Black people? Poor. Many Aframericans self-identify as poor. You are living in a reality that tells you that you have got nothing and you cannot get anything. Unless somebody parachutes in a good school, you cannot attend a good school. Unless somebody parachutes in a program to let you go to college, you cannot go to college. Unless somebody who does not look like you wants to marry you, you cannot have good children. Unless somebody else will do something for you, you do not exist. All you are getting is the reality created by people who despise you and want to control you—a nightmare. You have not created your own reality.

This lack of initiative, lack of self-empowerment, near-paralyzing fear of charting our own course because of the confusion that we have been taught bothers me. It bothers me because the only power that anyone has over me is the power I delegate to them. And I see unlimited power and potential in the Black community, which we are not using.

My solution has been to offer a whole range of economic self-empowerment proposals. Richard Poe's book *The Wave 4 Way to Building Your Downline* cites me for "urging Black Americans to lift themselves up through entrepreneurship"—especially direct sales and network marketing.[2] Dr. Ronald Fountain from Los Angeles is a tremendously successful network marketer.

In the mid-1980s I organized the Freedom campaign, an initiative to encourage Aframericans to spend their money within our own community. I have committed some of the data to memory: Every other ethnic group in America turns their money over in their own community from five to twelve times before one penny leaves. The average ethnic group recycles 80 percent of its income. Black America turns over each dollar less than once and spends only 4 percent of its income within its own community—and the percentage keeps falling. (Blacks recycled 7 percent of their money twenty years ago.)

The Freedom campaign was intended to get the Aframerican community to recycle its money. If you want to be equal in the United States, you cannot give other people 96 percent of your income and then blame them for 100 percent of your problems. You have got to take responsibility and build wealth in your own community.

We began the campaign with a Black History Month special on *Tony Brown's Journal* titled "The Color of Freedom," which presented a historical perspective on the need for economic self-determination and issued a call for spending money within the Black community. We even developed a currency, called the freedom, designed to build an Aframerican commercial system.

The concept was simple: There is no federal law against issuing your own money, and if you will accept my freedoms for your goods or services, I will accept yours—we will barter. If we get enough of us in a network that accepts freedoms, we can create a commercial system, in the same way the United States has created a commercial system based on the dollar. This concept has actually been successfully put into practice by a small group of people in Ithaca, New York.

We printed up the freedoms—you would be amazed how expensive it is to print money—and gave them out free of charge. People lined up to get them, but most kept them for souvenirs instead of using them as currency. So the freedom network never really took off.

Then, in the early 1990s, I came up with a different idea for building wealth in the Aframerican community. By that time, Black national organizations were spending hundreds of millions of dollars a year on conventions. I proposed that these organizations cancel their meetings one year, take a portion of the millions of dollars they would have spent on the conventions, and jointly buy twenty hotels in twenty urban markets. (Over 50 percent of Aframericans live in the top twenty urban areas.) These hotels would not only generate income but also create opportunities for Black people in those twenty markets to start businesses associated with the hospitality industry. This infrastructure would grow to sustain our national organizations and, through them, our community. Eventually, enough wealth would be created to develop funds to help people who need money to go to college, to take care of older people, and so on. (Immigrants from India, only 1.5 million in the United States, own 37 percent of all hotels and 52 percent of all motels in the country.)

Benjamin Hooks was the executive director of the NAACP at the time I proposed this idea. He brought together 150 heads of Black organizations and asked me to the address the gathering to see if we could get it off the ground. They were enthusiastic, many of them; but, sure enough, nobody would ever do anything.

It hurts, and I have to be honest, it has been hard to be patient when I could not get traction for what I (and countless other Blacks) consider sound ideas for economic self-empowerment of the Black community. I have had to work hard not to become permanently disillusioned. But, ultimately, these experiences have led me to the wisdom that while I consider it my moral obligation to preach the gospel of self-empowerment, nobody asked me to empower them. My failures have taught me patience because they have forced me to accept the reality that everybody is not at the same place and that everyone does not have the same consciousness, and being Black doesn't change that fact.

Over the years, Mama's value of patience has become clear to me: You have to allow other people to be who they are, rather than see them as reflections of yourself. Each of us is walking his or her own path. And only time can tell where these paths lead.

Patience and Perseverance

One thing is clear: We all suffer the consequences of our inaction. You cannot harvest what you did not plant. So, in the words of Suzanne De Passe, the celebrated producer and former president of Motown Productions, I have learned to take no as a vitamin. Mama's value of patience has helped me to focus on what I believe is right and to keep trying to build wealth in the Aframerican community.

The result of the competition between energies spent pursuing entitlement programs and energies spent developing pragmatic, market-driven social action is predictable: Blacks have lost economically and politically to Asians and Hispanics. "Their [Asians'] growing success has shifted power away from Blacks" is the way the USA Today headline stated the outcome of the one-sided competition.[3] "Blacks used to own 100 percent of the haircare retail market. Now they own perhaps 30 percent," Black Enterprise magazine reported.[4]

"Twenty years ago, blacks were No. 1 in U.S. minority business ownership. Not anymore. Now Hispanics are first, Asians second, and blacks third. . . . What's more, Asian businesses are bigger" ($336,200 annual revenue) than Hispanic ($155,200) and Black ($86,500) businesses.[5]

The result of this trend is a growing family income gap among Americans: Asians ($55,521), Whites ($45,904), Hispanics ($33,447), and Blacks ($30,439). With economic power, political power is also being redistributed. For example, Asian-Americans, 4 percent of the U.S. population, receive 12.2 percent of Small Business Administration–backed loans, while Aframericans, 12 percent of the U.S. population, get just 2.8 percent.[6]

You cannot build wealth if you cannot finance its development. Entitlement programs do not provide capital to build the community. That is why most of the buildings in Harlem are owned by non-Blacks, because we have not worked to give Aframericans the opportunity to own the homes they live in.

Why Blacks Are Losing Income and Homes (And How to Stop It)

The current housing predicament in Black neighborhoods began when Blacks missed the housing boom in their own backyard because of lending discrimination and misplaced priorities—in other words, emphasis on integration, busing, Ebonics, etc. Fads and 10 percent solutions consume energy; they do not solve 100 percent problems.

In the meantime, since the phenomenon of gentrification is playing itself out in such historic Black enclaves as Harlem and parts of Washington and Chicago, perhaps we should acknowledge and examine the difference between White gentrification and Black gentrification. A fascinating set of pressures and new data suggest that ownership is at the core of gentrification. Could you, for example, imagine a Chinatown without Chinese ownership or a Little Italy without Italian empowerment or Greek Town in Detroit without Greek gentrification? I cannot. Therefore, I submit, we should not accept the White gentrification of a Black community as the only model of multicultural progress and success.

Today, with White gentrification, not only do Blacks not own the commercially revitalized Harlem, but they are living in less of it because, increasingly, Blacks cannot afford to live there or in many other predominantly Black cities across the country. The high cost of renting has already precipitated an exodus of Blacks out of San Francisco, and in Princeton, New Jersey, Blacks are busy packing as well. What's worse, the dominant political scene in Black communities (unlike that of Asian ethnic groups, for example) is one of ineffectiveness and inattention to survival bread-and-butter issues such as entrepreneurship, household income, and home ownership. Black opinion leaders seem to be largely consumed by White racism, real and imagined, and oblivious to the fateful floodgate of overpopulation immigration that is taking away the very rental homes in which their constituents live, while it reduces their incomes as well. "From 1960 to 2000, the United States population increased 57 percent."[7] In the last ten years, the United States grew by the size of France. California alone is "growing by one person every minute."[8] (Some 10,000 new illegal immigrants enter the United States every day across the Mexican border.)

This 9/11 is an immigration bomb and the Aframerican community is at ground zero. However, in diffusing this socioeconomic threat, we should avoid resorting to either a racial resentment of immigrants by Whites or charges by Blacks that White opponents of overpopulation immigration are automatically racists. Racial and ethnic divisiveness only exacerbate this politically inspired predicament. The issue is not the nationality or color of the immigrants (because most of us are here as the result of some form of immigration), but the ability of the American infrastructure to absorb an excessive population growth and the economy's ability to provide prosperity for the burgeoning population. Overall, controlled immigration grows our economy, and immigrants have traditionally become productive citizens. The focus should be on our government's failure to protect the interests of the country's citi-

TONY BROWN

zens. As a result, the sheer number of foreigners, a revealing census study shows, hits Blacks and Latinos the hardest because they "have lower levels of educational attainment."[9]

The Census Bureau has recently provided the public with official evidence that the income disparity between the more prosperous and the poor in this country "has long been driven by immigration rates."[10] "The surprising drop in median income in New York City that has puzzled demographers studying the results of the 2000 census appears to be traceable in large part to immigration," *The New York Times* reported.[11] The *Times* said new Census Bureau data "show income declines concentrated heavily in neighborhoods . . . that have become magnets for new arrivals."[12]

Add the White middle-class gentrification of the Harlems of America—like the one led by Bill Clinton—to the army of poor immigrants who are settling in mostly Black cities such as Newark, Patterson, Princeton, and Trenton—all in New Jersey— and you get a housing crisis. Slowly, but surely, the Black population is evolving into a displaced and poorer community because of the insidious twins of racism and overpopulation. And the new census data report is proof that the government's strategy of increasing the illegal population through bipartisan amnesties and lax border security (to increase partisan political power) is borne on the backs of the lower one-third of Blacks and Latinos in poverty.

Social scientist and author Roy Beck and other experts on over-population immigration have been saying for years that, since the Civil War, new waves of European immigrants have pushed the lower one-third of Aframericans back into poverty just when they were about to escape into the middle class.[13] Here's the evidence from the Census Bureau that poor Blacks and Latinos, native-born people who have a high school degree or less and legal immigrants who obeyed the law (unlike the politicians), have been penalized economically and suffer from a growing income disparity linked to the educational level of Americans: Throughout New York City, incomes went up by 5.1 percent (to $59,155) for Whites and by 3.8 percent (to $72,145) for Asians. For Blacks, household incomes increased by just 1.1 percent, to $38,512. The incomes of Latinos also went up by only 1.1 percent, to $39,609.[14] The salient point is that even when incomes improved, "Blacks did less well," the *Times* said.[15] Latinos were a close second in the immigration-induced-income-disparity gap, which strongly suggests that whatever is depressing the household income of Blacks is doing the same to Latinos, and for the same reason (overpopulation immigration). Both marginal ethnic communities also bear the burden of serving as havens for most low-skilled and illiterate illegal immigrants. Perhaps this is why 67 percent of Latinos support tougher immigration laws, according to a Roper poll.[16]

The pressure of overpopulation is now a forgone conclusion. Half of the illegal immigrants come from Mexico, where all previous talk of stemming the migratory tide through better economics has ceased. Instead the Mexican government of Vicente Fox has issued a stunning new official report that said due to the lure of the minimum wage in the United States and the future guarantee of more long-range poverty in Mexico, the United States can expect an average of at least 400,000 new Mexican nationals per year (the legal quota for Mexican immigrants is 75,000) or conservatively about 5 million new immigrants every ten years.[17]

This official deception is a covert collaborative plan between the Mexican and United States governments, and because it is a stealth policy, neither government openly proposes a strategy for aiding the illegal nationals for fear of having its true motives exposed. But the strains in the system are increasingly apparent, as the social needs of the newcomers cannot be hidden—schools for the children they already have and those they will give birth to, jobs to sustain their families, health care, and affordable housing to shelter them. The cost of these services is enormous. Already U. S. taxpayers spend millions of dollars a year for their use of public assistance, which inadvertently gives an unfair competitive advantage to businesses that employ them as cheap labor.

Returning these people to Mexico as a solution is out of the question and not politically possible because our government is unofficially importing them, as it undermines the rule of law. The crisis, therefore, is locked into the system and protected by the government—which, ironically, refuses to pay the social services tab. The only viable and humane option is to support those already here while getting our immigration policy in perspective and under control. Many of the politicos of both parties will not be helpful because they see Latino immigration as a way to increase the numbers of voters for their partisan benefit. Succinctly, over-population immigration is a government-sponsored program.

The "Community of Spirit" Solution

Therefore, government relief for the Aframerican and other victims of this policy is not forthcoming. They will have to fend for themselves with an out-of-the-box market solution to increase their incomes and equity through home ownership. In a word, self-empowerment.

Aframericans need to rewrite the notion of progress and success, then reflect it in a sensible empowerment strategy that stresses the ownership of homes and rental properties, so those residents displaced by skyrocketing rents and the average Black person who wants to participate will also have something to show for gentrification—as they come to realize that houses could be better investments than stocks. (Housing prices have exploded, with annual gains of nearly 10 percent.) The alternative to this idea of self-empowerment is to remain as inside-the-box prisoners of the status quo who are further marginalized by economic exclusion and, ultimately, poverty.

So, as usual, Black people are on their own to once again demonstrate that Harlem, New York, is, as one writer put it, "a place that held itself together through good times and bad by its community of spirit."[18] If Blacks' ancestors could survive with this "community of spirit" under extremely restrictive circumstances, today's Aframericans should be able, under comparatively lenient circumstances, and with the same gene pool, to thrive just as creatively.

In that spirit and genre, let me suggest that since this housing predicament has created a profit bonanza for the landlords, the most viable solution is to become one, especially your own—and, perhaps, become a millionaire. Therefore, I, along with mortgage bankers Harold Ford and Julian Ford, call this solution The Millionaires' Club, a program to show people that real estate is the best investment for the average person because it is an intergenerational transfer of wealth that prevents the next generation of children from going into poverty once the parents die. Traditionally, few Black children inherit any form of capital wealth. Breaking the poverty cycle with inherited wealth is a market solution of necessity for Aframericans because of overpopulation immigration and White gentrification, and the timing could not be better.

In "the remarkable January" of 2002, home sales soared as they set a record annualized rate, the first ever above 6 million.[19] Even during 2001, when the terror attacks on September 11 stalled home sales, as well as the nation's economy, Americans still bought more homes than in any previous year.[20] After a five-year boom, the housing market in cities significantly appreciated, and "the investment risk seems minimal," advised *USA Today*.[21] In fact, the housing market looks like the booming stock market of the late 1990s.[22] By October 2002, the remarkable drop in home financing costs and the monthly payment on a new mortgage were the cheapest in thirty-one years. The *USA Today* business page headline declared: "Rising Home Values Have Made Houses More Appealing Investments Than Stocks."[23]

Ninety percent of millionaires in America got their money from real estate, and we have discovered the reasons why. So, to help those who are disadvantaged and discriminated against by the traditional housing market, or simply unaware of its potential, two young Black mortgage bankers, Harold and Julian Ford, whom I mentor, have developed an empowerment-housing program. They acquire a house; they provide the financing for the purchaser for the loan; and then they sell the purchaser an income-producing property.

The new owner can live mortgage-free in one unit, while using the money from the other one or two units to pay off the monthly note. If there is anything left, the owner keeps it. The Fords also teach the new owner how to find government-guaranteed tenants to ensure a reliable cash flow and provide management services to help the inexperienced. This turnkey "millionaires'" plan is intended to get one house a year for ten years for each qualified family in our community. In the New York–New Jersey real estate market, the empowered owner can have $1.5 million or more in equity.

Thus, if the average person or a family can buy an income-producing property once a year, in ten years they can accumulate enough assets to be financially independent. In that way, the economically borderline and disadvantaged members of the community who can be qualified by this process, as well as those in the more fortunate higher income group, can become rich and wealthy.

Like this millionaires' club, the Aframerican community's self-empowerment must come from market-driven solutions (empowerment through entrepreneurship) that can be applied to just about every social or economic predicament. One such program that I developed involves the sale of Grenadian spices and personal care products to raise funds for a non-profit foundation in Texas to benefit needy Aframerican children and to create the Rebuild The Black Wall Street Fund for the Greenwood Business District in Tulsa, which was destroyed by the Tulsa Race Riot of 1921—eighty-two years ago.

How patient can you get? I thought that since I broke the story on national TV in 1972, and since the Greenwood district is still lagging in economic opportunity, perhaps I'm the right person to come up with a solution to a decades-old predicament.

And since our ancestors built a Black Wall Street over eighty years ago, I told the audience at the memorial service for the eighty-first anniversary of the Tulsa Race Riot that we obviously have the inherent ability to excel: "You cannot lose sight of the fact that the skills and the talent and the wonderful integrity of the men and women who built Greenwood have been passed along to you." Therefore, self-empowerment is the essential ingredient in any market solution. "Do It Again" is my challenge to Blacks.

Time is running out on Aframericans, and they are being left in the dust of the new immigrant groups that are excelling at the economic opportunities offered in the United States. Mama taught me that patience and perseverance are essential elements of success. Throughout my public career, I have drawn strength from this conviction.

As many times as I have been wrong, I needed some victories to keep me going, a kind of patience builder. One reminder came from a man in Sacramento. He bought my 1997 book *Empower the People* in 2002 and wrote, "Reading your book was like reading the current headlines. Man, you are scary about what you said about IMF, and other information, what you said in 1997. You said you don't claim to be a prophet, but the Bible says if it comes to pass that would be a sign of a prophet!" I don't consider myself a prophet, but I did predict in that 1997 book that oil (then under $20 a barrel) was headed toward $50 a barrel. I was laughed at to my face by the "experts." However, as I finished this book in 2002, the price of oil had increased—between March and September by 45 percent—to well over $30 a barrel, as it steadily moved into the $50 neighborhood.

This gain came mainly from the fundamentals that I previously explained (mostly the new demand for oil from two new industrial giants—China and India, about half of the world's population), but boosted also by Iraq war talk and the Saudi Arabia–led OPEC cartel's ability to deliberately keep oil prices artificially high—as a hostile act against the Western world and the United States specifically, which is why it is so scary that the United States refuses to break its oil dependency on Saudi Arabia and develop a renewable source of energy (i.e., a hydrogen-fueled economy). Therefore, the future supply of oil (that controls our lives) will remain tight because of the uncertainty of war and America's constant wars with someone in the Gulf region over oil for years to come. Depending on how a war with Iraq turns out, the $50-a-barrel spike (economic catastrophe) could materialize as surely as the new higher prices that I also predicted in 1997 for gold and silver did in 2002. This minor insight feeds my faith in other areas.

I know in my heart that economic self-determination is the only true path to self-empowerment for Black people or any other group. It is time that Aframericans tried something new, or did something old that works. I also know in my head that Aframericans know it too—because the number of Black-owned firms has increased almost four times faster than the number of all U.S. firms in the last ten years. The $645.9 billion of Black spending power is also larger than the $580.5 billion of U.S. Latino spending power, but not for long.

The Latino population is growing faster and they are translating their business success into political clout, in a big way. They will emerge in a couple of decades as a strategic political powerhouse. Unfortunately, Aframericans did not utilize the strategy that I explained in *Black Lies, White Lies* about controlling the presidential vote by exploiting the electoral college process. But Latinos will automatically implement it—because their population grew by 60 percent between 1990 and 2002 and mainly because it is concentrated in seven of the nine pivotal electoral college states that elect the president of the United States: Florida, California, Texas, New York, New Jersey, Illinois, and Pennsylvania. Furthermore, by 2020, Latinos will comprise 21 percent of the U.S. population.

As I said earlier, I was recently chosen to be the CEO of UATV, which challenges me to combine my long-standing belief in community empowerment, utilizing, in this instance, media as a means of mass distribution for aspiring entrepreneurs who normally cannot afford it. (See Chapter 5 for details.)

A survey reported that 21 percent of those currently in the

workforce who are likely to leave their jobs (three in ten people) want to start a business.[24] Ronald Langston, director of the Minority Business Development Agency (MBDA) of the U.S. Department of Commerce, has even adopted the theme: "Empowerment Through Entrepreneurship." The UATV network will endeavor to help as many individuals as possible who seek self-empowerment through information and small businesses (some home-based) gain a media outlet for their products and services. Hopefully, they will be motivated to succeed, despite the odds.

Put another way, this plan assumes a basic belief in people and it provides a financial incentive for everyone who will do the right thing. UATV will benefit greatly if it helps aspiring entrepreneurs. Doing well while doing good is good, especially when a historically suppressed group is offered the chance-of-a-lifetime opportunity to help and empower itself. The combination of community empowerment and corporate profits becomes greater than the sum of its parts if one drives the other in a cycle of mutual dependence and opportunity.

The Rewards of Patience

In the spring of 2001, John Chase, president of the Augusta, Georgia, chapter of the Black Data Processing Association (BDPA), greeted me at the airport a few hours before I was to speak at BDPA's annual event. On the way to the hotel, we talked about a variety of issues and how they affected Aframericans. The main thrust was closing the income inequality and the information technology gaps between Aframericans and Latinos on the bottom and Asian-Americans at the very top, followed by Whites—the paradigm of the newly emerging American class system of digital haves and have-nots. Family income, which I mentioned earlier, follows the same pattern as technology proficiency.

Amid the serious conversation, as we drove past it, John pointed out the golf course on which the annual Masters tournament takes place and asked with a twinkle in his eyes, "What did you call a group of White men with clubs chasing a Black man in Augusta fifty years ago?"

"A lynch mob," I answered.

"Correct. What do you call a group of White men with clubs who are chasing a Black man in Augusta today?"

"What?"

"The Masters."

"There has never been a golfer like this, in this country or the world, white or black," the New York sportswriter Mike Lupica exclaimed.[25] He made that statement as Tiger Woods won the 102nd U.S. Open "with style . . . grace . . . and grit."[26] "I'm only twenty-six," Woods reminded us.

The exchange with John and the words of Lupica reminded me how far Aframericans have come, how much the world has changed. Even though it has often seemed to me that things were not moving fast enough, we have made tremendous progress in America. The progress of individual Aframericans is probably wider and deeper than most people suspect. And, because that progress was earned, it is permanent.

I am very proud of Black people for overcoming the obstacles of institutional racism. White America has also come a long way in freeing itself of racist attitudes—they are just no longer tolerated. Young White people are more open than any generation has ever been, so we know we are going in the right direction.

"If you study physics twenty-four hours a day," I used to say in my speeches in the early 1990s, "you'll be a physicist; if you study chemistry twenty-four hours a day, you'll be a chemist; and if you study racism twenty-four hours a day, you'll be a racist. . . . White people, the Congress, civil rights bills, affirmative action bills, nothing is going to change our status but that ultimate decision that we must make within us that we are as good as anybody else in this society."

It is apparent that a lot of Black people have made that decision. For example, since 1999, three Black men have become chief executive officers of American icons among the Fortune 50 companies. Kenneth I. Chenault ascended to become chief executive officer of American Express. Another Black man, E. Stanley O'Neal, became the chief executive officer at Merrill Lynch, and a third, Richard Dean Parsons, became the chief executive officer of AOL Time Warner, the largest and most powerful media company in the world. There was enough Black power in mainstream United States business for *Fortune* to run a cover story entitled "The 50 Most Powerful Black Executives in America."[27]

The successes of Aframericans are extending into every area of endeavor. Until 2002, Hollywood had turned a blind eye on the talents of Black actors: No Black woman had ever won an Oscar for best actress, and only one Black man, Sidney Poitier, had won the best actor award, in 1963. On March 24, 2002, history was made at the 74th Academy Awards when both the best actor and the best actress awards went to Aframericans. Denzel Washington attributed his achievement to good acting. A tearful Halle Berry saw herself mostly as a symbol who had opened a door that had been shut to Black women throughout Hollywood's racially impenitent history.

I am convinced that Washington and Berry will continue to win awards, leading the way for other Black actors, because they are superbly skillful. Washington's and Berry's Oscars are the real thing, given not for Black or White performances but for achievement at the top of human potential.

I believe that we are moving, however gradually, to where skills and accomplishments—not race—are the measure of success. "I cannot absorb living in a world where I have an Oscar for best actress," said Julia Roberts before the Academy Awards, "and Denzel doesn't have one for best actor."[28] I believe that some Whites are further down the road to accepting Blacks than some Blacks are to accepting themselves. The door of opportunity is now wide open, and Hollywood's history of racism is flat on its back—as long as Blacks commit themselves to being the best. The true historic first on March 24, 2002, was that Americans opened their eyes and minds to the wisdom within them, that America won.

And we will continue winning as long as we keep our minds open. The signs are everywhere. When Indiana won the South Regional basketball championship, students waved posters that read: "Knight-time is over, it's a new Da-vis!" in honor of their new, winning Black coach, Mike Davis, who succeeded the legendary Bobby Knight.[29]

Early in 2002, Tyrone Willingham was named the head football coach at the University of Notre Dame. "When I was a kid," wrote Bob Herbert in *The New York Times,* "you could no more imagine a black person running the football program at Notre Dame than you could imagine, say, a black secretary of state."[30]

Of course, America now has not only a Black secretary of state in Colin Powell but also a Black woman national security adviser. It is significant to note that a 2001 Gallup Poll named Colin Powell the second most admired man in America, right after the president of the United States. The same poll named Condoleezza Rice the fifth most admired American woman.[31] (There is speculation in official circles, according to media reports, that President George W. Bush may court history in 2004 by nominating Condoleezza Rice as Vice President Dick Cheney's replacement, and if she is elected, Rice would automatically become the front-runner for the Republican presidential nomination in 2008.)

I have already mentioned Tiger Woods, the leading golfer in the world. Two of the top female tennis players on the international tour are Venus and Serena Williams; they met in the first all-sister Wimbledon final in 118 years when they faced each other in 2002 (Serena won). The 2002 Games in Salt Lake City have given us bobsledder Vonetta Flowers, the first U.S. Black athlete to win a gold medal at the Winter Olympics, who was promptly joined by bobsled teammates Randy Jones and Garrett Hines, the first U.S. Black male athletes to win medals in Winter Olympics sports.

I am listing not Black achievement but achievement that is at the top of human potential. History has proved Mama right. The day has arrived when young Black children have a whole range of heroes—not just Joe Louis—to choose from. Social change can be observed only as a trend line. But that gradual progress is wide and deep, says Halle Berry.

"Indeed, there is no major area of American life these days, from education to politics to religion," declared *Newsweek* in a cover story entitled "The New Color of Power," "where society is not coming to terms with a new black leadership class—one whose credentials, in many cases, have very little to do with their color, and one whose very existence raises questions about the continuing viability of the 'black leadership' model of old."[32]

It is a noteworthy characteristic of most of the members of this "new black leadership class" that they see themselves in terms that transcend race. "I think that's [race is] a narrow definition of a person because it's only one element of who they are," E. Stanley O'Neal of Merrill Lynch told *Newsweek*.[33] The magazine, in fact, poses the following question: "So how should we view these men— as black CEOs, or CEOs who happen to be black?" Why not humans with an African ancestry who happen to be Americans?

Colin Powell, in a February 14, 2002, appearance on MTV's Global Forum, gave a fascinating insight into how some of the new Black leaders see themselves. "I consider myself an African-American, a Black man," Secretary Powell said in answer to a young woman who asked him what he meant when he once commented to an interviewer, "I ain't that Black." "As I go about my job, what I say to people is, 'I'm the American secretary of state.' I don't say 'I'm the Black secretary of state,' because that implies, 'Gee, is there a White one somewhere?' "[34]

Condoleezza Rice, Powell's friend and colleague in the White House, took the thought a step further. "Throughout my life, I've tried to encourage young Black people to have unlimited horizons and to seek education as a way to approach those horizons," she told *Essence* magazine. "But in the final analysis, I'm the national security adviser of the United States. I'm not the Black national security adviser of the United States. And I have to do my job to carry out the interests of the United States. Since I believe that the United States is the most successful multiethnic democracy ever known on the face of the earth, I think in pursuing the interests of the United States I'm doing an awful lot for multiethnic democracy and the spread of multiethnic democracy worldwide."[35]

Clearly, these highly accomplished people want to be acknowledged as leaders rather than as "Black leaders." "The old labels have lost a lot of their meaning," says Harold Ford, Jr., a Democratic congressman from Tennessee. "Rigid ideology makes it easier to resist good ideas."[36]

I believe that it is no accident that the Black people who are rising to the pinnacles of achievement are those who judge themselves in human terms, first and foremost. When internal racial barriers no longer hold us back, discrimination truly comes to an end, and we are free to pursue health, wealth, and happiness.

I have waited a long time, sometimes impatiently, to see Aframericans liberate themselves from the vestiges of self-hatred, a subtle psychological process learned from centuries of hate and oppression. The seeds of hope and faith that Mama planted in my heart helped light my way and expose the truth. And the rewards of patience are great—the joy of witnessing the perseverance of the human spirit.

Yet, there is more work to be done. As each of us connects with our humanity, we must share it with our brothers and sisters. In the next chapter, we will look at how you can create health, wealth, and happiness in your community by sharing your love.

$\mathcal{L}ove$

7
THE VALUE OF LIVING JOYFULLY

A little while ago, I accompanied a camera crew on a shoot in a children's AIDS ward at a local hospital. As we went about our business, the children seemed particularly interested in the cameraman. At first I thought they were fascinated by the equipment he carried. But as I watched the children reach out and take hold of the man, I realized that they were seeing in him a human warmth, a source of love.

Many of the children had been in the hospital since they were infants, and they were hungry for human contact. They wanted to be held. And, with unfailing instinct, they picked out the man from whom they could get some of the love they needed so much.

The children literally hung on the man, clutching him around the legs, arms, and neck. The cameraman just glowed as the children clung to him, delighted to share his love with them. The expression on his face reminded me so much of Mama. For a moment, I was transported back into her arms.

"I love you, Sonny Boy," she said to me every day, often adding, "I am so lucky to have you."

There has never been a day when I have doubted Mama's love. That is why I am so blessed. I was born into enormous wealth. It was just a matter of time before I got money. You see, love, not money, is the cornerstone of life. It is the foundation of success, of self-empowerment, of freedom, and even of the economic progress of groups and nations. Giving and receiving love, we are joined to the universal consciousness of all creation—we experience the true joy of our humanity.

"People are foolish not to love one another," Mama would say. Now, as I near the end of my own journey, I understand what she meant. It was not the naïve belief of an unquestioningly religious woman but the wisdom of a magnificent spirit. The simple statement sums up Mama's value of love: Share your love, and it will come back to you a thousandfold as health, wealth, and happiness.

Finding the Love You Need

A defining characteristic of my relationship with Mama was that she never tried to pretend to be something she was not. From the moment I was old enough to understand, she told me about my biological family and about how I came to live with her. Although I was too young to articulate it, I always knew that Mama had made a choice to love me. She did not give birth to me. I was not her flesh and blood, and yet this woman sacrificed for me like I was the only child in the world, a special gift from God.

There was Mama in midlife, having a hard enough time taking care of herself. She had already raised a daughter, Mabel. What would compel her to accept—in fact, to seek out—the emotional and economic burden of raising someone else's child? The only answer that makes any sense is love. It was the principle she lived by, convinced that love is the conduit to that oneness, that place we all come from and return to.

Mama's love, because it was given freely and not out of a feeling of obligation, filled me with a true sense of security. No matter what happened, I believed, love would find me, the way Mama had found me. It was just a given that, no matter what else I lacked for, I would always have love.

Over the years, especially in my time as a psychiatric social worker, I have seen lots of people who did not get enough love as children. Some people were not held enough. Others did not get enough approval. Still others felt rejected by their families. Many of these people have come to believe that they did not get the love they wanted from their biological parents because they are not worthy. It is easy to see why economic security and educational achievement do not insulate people from emotional breakdowns.

My experience with Mama taught me that everybody is worthy and that there is enough love in the world for all of us. As I grew and learned more about our community, this belief was further reinforced. In Charleston, the custom was that if a child's biological parents were unable to care for the child, someone else stepped in. The Black community saw the children as a responsibility for all, and many children were raised by people other than their parents. For a whole community to commit itself to the well-being of every child takes a big love. In Charleston, we grew up nourished by the love of the whole proverbial "village."

As a result, I learned to recognize and accept love. For example, my father was not a part of my life, but I found wonderful surrogates. I found myself adopting fathers. In elementary school, there was Mr. Carpenter, who was the only man in the school. Mr. Carpenter was the principal, and he was this good-looking, distinguished guy, with salt-and-pepper hair, three-piece suits, a gold watch, and a Phi Beta Kappa key. He looked like a Black Clark Gable. Although he was strict, it was clear that Mr. Carpenter really cared about all of us and our futures.

Then, in junior high school, there was the track coach and the principal, Mr. Preston. He had been a naval officer in World War II and had a real modern air about him. In high school, there was Mr. Barnes, the English literature teacher and, most important, my drama mentor. It made me so proud to see these good-looking, well-dressed, intelligent Black men devoting their professional lives to educating Black children.

Mr. Andrew Calloway, the superintendent of Negro schools, my friend Scotty's dad, was another surrogate father. He used to take Scotty and me and a few of our other buddies swimming at the local Black college. Few of us had fathers like Scotty's, who intentionally stepped in and mentored us.

Then there was Horace, Mabel's boyfriend. He was a truck driver. Horace would go all over the state to make deliveries to various warehouses and stores. Sometimes, I rode in his big truck with him, and boy, that was exciting. I helped him unload the truck, and we had lunch together. He was really nice to me, very caring.

So by the time Mama made her transition to the next world

when I was twelve, I had this foundation of love. I was surrounded by a whole loving community that gave me confidence in myself and the world.

This was not an easy time. I went to live with my biological mother. Billie and my brother Nathan were also living with her. My birth mother was never well equipped emotionally for nurturing, so my oldest sister, Billie, who was six years older than I was, took it upon herself to care for me. Billie and I were like identical twins, and with the exact same personality. She made sure that I was fed and did my homework. She taught me about the world, about the birds and the bees, about people. She really looked out for me, and I looked up to her and loved this angel the same way I loved Mama.

Everything I am and everything I have accomplished is the product of the love I have found throughout my life. There have always been teachers, mentors, family members (including my brother Nathan and sister Jackie), and friends who have given of themselves so freely, with such joy. They have been my inspiration for devoting my life to the cause of justice, truth, and self-empowerment.

I would be remiss if I did not mention Dr. H. Naylor Fitzhugh, formerly the vice president for special markets at Pepsi-Cola Company, my TV sponsor for over twenty years and the first corporate sponsor of a Black national television series. He was my mentor and guided me through my professional life for years. I met him when I was still in Detroit running my little public relations business, and he was very generous with his time and knowledge. Dr. Fitzhugh, a former professor at Howard University's School of Business and Administration, was a real giant and pioneer in the Aframerican business community. Anywhere you turn today, the people he mentored are at the top of their fields.

And, finally, there was Mick Colgan, one of the greatest, most decent human beings I have ever encountered. Mick was the in-house television and studio director at NET when I started with *Black Journal*. He directed the *MacNeil/Lehrer NewsHour*. He directed Bill Moyers. All the top shows.

Mick did not do anything for public recognition. He did not do anything to get you to like him. He just went about his business, always with a touch of green in his attire to bring out his Irish pride, helping all of us make our shows look good. All of us on *Black Journal/Tony Brown's Journal* were learning as we went along, and Mick spent hours and hours helping us figure out what shots to use, how to mix the sound. He did not have to be there, and yet he would stay with us throughout the edit sessions, often until four or five in the morning. Mick really wanted our show to be a success. He was just a wonderful human being.

My relationship with Mick was a truly transformative one. At a time when I saw everything in terms of race, Mick's love allowed me to get to know a White person as a human being. It was the Mick Colgans of my life, the Bob Freedmans, the Gerry Sallans, the Bill Kobins, and the Don Dixons who have helped me grow into a better person. These White people never asked me to be someone other than who I was. They were not threatened by me. They accepted me as a Black person who believed that the sun set and rose in Black people. They did not let that deter them from treating me as a human being. They could make this leap into humanity because they were not afraid to identify themselves beyond being White.

Quite frankly, their love wore me down. Through their love I returned to what Mama had taught me and what was already inside me, that it was foolish for people not to love one another. I learned to practice what Martin Luther King preached and judged people by their character and not the color of their skin. Once you do that, human beings make sense.

We all want to be loved, to be seen and accepted for who we are. When we feel that we have not gotten the love we want, many of us begin to look for love in unhealthy ways. When human beings do not share love with one another, it is not too long before they turn on one another. "When the bins are empty, the horses bite one another," Dr. Fitzhugh used to tell me.

Of one thing we may be sure: The tragedy of 9/11 has forced us to learn a larger lesson—to understand why 3,000 innocent people died so tragically. On September 11, 2002, one year later, the planetary energies of the heavens paid their respects to these martyrs. Those energies told us that their ultimate sacrifice was made so the world could realize that we are one family of humanity caught up in foolish ancient and obsolete allegiances to various cultural conditionings.

The lesson is that universal selfishness and a failure to understand one another lie at the heart of global strife. Therefore, we Americans must avenge our dead with justice and restraint. Until the world changes from its deepest depth of consciousness the slaughter of innocents throughout the world will continue. In order to break this cycle, collective humanity must be integrated into mature psyches. Ultimately, we are all accountable for our handling of our world and all of its creatures. Love, mercy, and a higher spiritual idealism will evolve through the grief and memories of devastation. Ultimately, the human family will become conscious of itself.

The threat of terrorism can truly be halted only by our ability as a human family to show our love for one another by creating societies that are egalitarian and just and by focusing all religions on tolerance. The only reason we have poverty and oppression in the world is that not enough of us love one another enough to help our brothers and sisters start down the path of self-empowerment. And I believe that the reason for much of this emotional poverty is that many people—rich and poor—feel that they did not get enough love when they were growing up.

I offer a simple solution: Mama. The same love that she gave me, she would gladly have shared with anyone who needed it. She would have loved you, too. As long as you draw breath, you can breathe in the healing power of love. Start with Mama, take strength in her love, then find other people in your life who will give you the love you need. And then share the wealth.

Putting Love to Work

I started out seeing the world as a Black person, and now, thanks to the love I have been blessed with, I see the world as a human being. From that perspective, what I see is that we are all members of the human family. I also see that we are still blinded by the Hegelian dialectic of "race," which the Establishment has used to maintain its hold on power. Love is the true path to self-empowerment.

On the one hand, if you see the human family as different races, then you have to take sides. All there is instead of cooperation is self-interest, suspicion, and mistrust. Stereotypes replace real understanding, and division takes the place of mutual respect.

On the other hand, if you see the whole human race as your family, you will work to feed, protect, educate, and enrich every member of that family. Universal affirmative action becomes the only kind of preference that makes sense. You will cooperate with the other family members to create wealth, to build human capital, to educate the children, to look after old people, to give everyone an opportunity to share in the blessings of health, wealth, and happiness.

That is the payoff of seeing ourselves as a family: plenty of health, wealth, and happiness to go around. We have the potential for such plenty, and yet the majority of our brothers and sisters are starving, because we do not love one another. We are divided by the belief that we belong to different families or different races and are ready to kill one another in the name of our "race," our political beliefs, and, increasingly, our religion.

That is because the core problem in the world today is the scarcity of love. If we put aside our differences, we would have the opportunity and the foundation to build successful economic models for everyone. We could build greater wealth for the whole world, erasing some of the disparity between the haves and the have-nots.

Yes, love can build a foundation for peace and prosperity. I have come to understand this transformative power of love over thirty years of striving to bring the message of self-empowerment to the Aframerican community in this country. I always put being Black in the context of being an American. Self-empowerment, in my mind, was a way to make the country better. The ultimate goal was reconciliation. However, there could be reconciliation, I knew, only if Black people made themselves equal.

I never did believe that I was inferior, and I never wanted Black people to believe themselves to be inferior in order to be accepted, which is what the assimilationists' doctrine (integration) demands. "You can be mediocre," it tells Black people, "and we will tell you

you're going to be successful." That is not love, it is at best indifference, and at worst hatred.

You cannot succeed if you are mediocre. Mediocrity is going to catch up with you, sooner or later. If a young person does not have the skills to get through Harvard but is accepted because of his or her race, that person is bound to fail and to lose confidence in the process. There is no sense in going to Harvard just to graduate with a degree in self-doubt. That will not make you successful in life. Many graduates of elitist schools prove that fact every day. Accepting yourself and excelling at being yourself is what makes people successful.

All along, I was doing Mama's work. The way Mama had taught me to read by asking me to read the store signs in downtown Charleston, I have tried to show Black people how to empower themselves. Mama always taught me that nothing succeeded like success. She gave me confidence in myself, because she encouraged me to compete and to earn what I got.

What I have tried to show the Aframerican community is that nobody other than you can make you free or equal or happy. Moreover, people can have a productive relationship only as equals. If you love yourself for who you are and I love myself for who I am, we can love each other. Love is based on trust, and there can be no trust between people who are filled with self-doubt or self-hatred.

We will never be really free if we keep looking to someone else to create our success reality. Freedom is based on power. Power is based on wealth. And wealth can be created only through true universal affirmative action.

I am going to say that again, another way. Affirmative action creates wealth. Wealth creates power. And power creates freedom (and the color of freedom is green).

My universal affirmative action program comes out of the Holy Bible. It is the Parable of the Prodigal Son. The parable tells the story of a father with two sons. They have a prosperous business. The younger son decides that he wants to go out into the world to have some fun. He takes the money that his father gives him, goes out, and blows it on booze and girls and partying. Subsequently, he realizes that he has done wrong and returns home to seek forgiveness. The father is elated. He kills the fatted calf and holds a celebration for the prodigal son. The older son is livid. "Why," he asks, "do you honor the son who went against your wishes?" The father, in his wisdom, responds, "Your brother was lost, and now he is found. He was dead, and now he is alive," meaning the family had grown by one.[1]

You can strengthen the chain only by strengthening the weakest link in the chain. In the event this is all a little too spiritual for your tastes, let me explain how it works in hard, cold, capitalistic, free-enterprise terms. The National Basketball Association (NBA) is a quintessential universal affirmative action program. At the end of the season, which team in the NBA gets the best new player? The weakest. The worst team. Believe it or not, there is a very good business reason why they put that eight-foot player who makes fifty points a game on the team that has not won a game all season. When you put the best player on the worst team, chances are higher that on any given day or night any team in the league can defeat any other team. That way, the overall league is more competitive. And if the overall league is more competitive, more of us watch it on television. The television networks then charge advertisers higher fees and pay higher fees to the owners of the teams. The owners of the teams, in turn, pay higher wages to the players. It is win-win only when you strengthen the weakest link in the chain. When adopted, that kind of affirmative action is universally fair and beneficial for all of us, and it helps heal the nation.

I did not say "if" adopted, but "when," because the United States has already demonstrated the validity of my theory and the practicality of the biblical parable. We have prosperity in America today largely because of universal affirmative action. The most successful affirmative action program that we have ever had was a preference program called the G.I. Bill. After World War II, we gave all the men and women (mostly White men) who had served in the armed forces money to go to college. As a result, we had all of these young people who would never have gone to college become college graduates. They became the foundation of today's middle class. We built America's middle class on preference, through a program for deserving veterans. And it worked. It could work again—if we loved one another.

Preference does not work when it is based on race alone, because it is not based on real need. However, once you accept that the only race is the human race, you come to the inescapable conclusion that every person in this society is equally precious. How can I choose between a Black child on the south side of Chicago or in Harlem and a White child in Appalachia or vice versa? I will never be compromised morally in that political paradox—the very Hegelian doctrine that enslaves Blacks and Whites. I do not want to argue that one child is more in need than another just because of the color of his or her skin (the result of a genetic sunburn caused by only six of forty thousand genes). Morally, we definitely cannot choose between them. The future is not about Black people and White people, it is about the human family.

Why can we not be a society in which no White child and no Black child is without a computer? Why can we not have an affirmative action program in America that ensures that no elderly person goes without care or dies alone—in pain? Because we have not created that reality of love. We are too busy arguing over the pseudo "race" reality—a reality created by haters, by people who prospered from slavery and segregation. We have been living in hell, and we have not changed that reality to a success reality in which all of us can do anything we want to do.

The reason the Black community does not have freedom is that we do not practice affirmative action within our own borders. And one of the big reasons we do not practice affirmative action is that we as a community have bought into the W. E. B. Du Bois misconstruction of the Talented Tenth. This concept is that you invest all your resources in the top 10 percent—the ones who are already successful or supposedly the most likely to succeed. Well, if you think about it, that is like building a pyramid with the point in the ground and the wide base in the air. How long do you think that kind of structure would withstand the natural elements?

We have to learn from the wisdom of the ancient Egyptians in Alkebu-Lan (Africa is the Roman term). They built pyramids that have stood for thousands of years. They built them with big bases firmly planted in the ground. That is the way to build a community—from its base up. You build a community and push everybody out of the bottom into the middle and as many people out of the middle into the top as you can. The more people who have something, the happier all of us are going to be. The more educated people you get, the more prosperous our society is going to be.

We have to free ourselves from the illusion of race and start building a reality of empowerment. We need affirmative action for needy people. I have adopted the definition of a needy person as "anyone who wants to help himself or herself," as taught by my friend Prime Minister Keith Mitchell of Grenada.

We should not have entitlement programs for rich people. What are the well-off people being compensated for—for being well-off? We should have a program for people who need help. No matter who or what they are. No matter what the color of their skin. That is how you create wealth.

Wealth comes in three forms. The first form of wealth is money. The second form of wealth is unity. It is called social capital—the ability of a person or a group to have high self-esteem, to feel capable to compete and to succeed and build institutions to aid other members of the community. The people who emigrate to the United States do not normally come with money. They come with an abundance of social capital. You see them live together. You see them work long hours. You then see them save money, lend money to one another, and send over for other family members. That is social capital. That is one form of wealth they bring with them.

Here is a quintessential example of social capital among Asian-Americans: Twelve business owners will contribute a thousand dollars each to a fund that is loaned on a handshake to a new immigrant entrepreneur, interest free. It is done to support Asian businesses, not because of friendship. Groups such as Aframericans where this tradition is unheard of or groups that are unwilling to adopt this tradition cannot compete with practitioners of such wealth creation.

The third form of wealth—human capital—is the greatest. Human capital is the sum of your formal education and your learned work experience. When you combine your human capital (your wisdom) with your social capital (your willingness to build your community), money is an inevitable by-product. With your love added to this equation, your wealth becomes a success reality. All you are turning out now is young people and old people—people willing to help themselves—who can be productive and successful.

We can spend day and night amassing material riches, but until we build real wealth by investing our love in each member of the human family, we will not have peace and prosperity in our nation or in the world. Unity, the experience of being one with the universal consciousness, is the key to spiritual health, wealth, and happiness.

The Rewards of Love

A man approached me once at a conference and asked, "Mr. Brown, are you married?" I said, "I will answer the question for you if you will answer one for me." He agreed. I said, "So, I will answer your question. I am not married. Now, you tell me, are you married?" "Yes, I am married," the man replied. "Are you happy?" I continued, in response to which he changed the subject. "Why didn't you ask me if I was happy?" I asked. "If you had asked that, I would have said yes."

I am happy because I love my work. (I believe that truly happy people cannot tell the difference between work and play.) I have had to sacrifice much in my life for this love. I admire, and even envy a little, people who know how to balance their professional and personal lives. I tried marriage; it did not work. My desire to leave the world a bit better than I found it has always come first, often at the price of other commitments. The reward, however, is that I know that I have invested my life in a labor of love.

Not a day goes by without someone telling me about the difference I have made in his or her life. "Dear Mr. Brown," wrote one viewer in a recent e-mail message. "For years, I have watched you on TV. You have been an inspiration in my life. Thanks to people like yourself, I am now getting ready to graduate with a history major and a minor in social science. Whether you know it or not, you have made a difference in my life. Thank you for your contribution to our nation and to minority advancement." This is the repayment of my love, and there can be no greater wealth.

Tony Brown's Journal's ratings demonstrate both a broad geographic and culturally diverse acceptance—for example, the series performs above average in such culturally distinct markets as multiethnic New York City, Middle America Oklahoma City, Southwestern Albuquerque, and very White Salt Lake City, just to name a few. This suggests that prideful Blacks identify with the program as being relevant to their lives and that the above-average acceptance among Whites seems to stem from their perception, as many have told me over the years, and what a White housewife from Linden, Alabama, wrote in an e-mail the day I was finishing this section of the book: "Tony, I have watched your PBS program for years, mainly because I wanted to understand Black people." Another typical show response from this demographic group arrived the same day from a high school principal in Toronto, Ontario: "The message was wonderful for ALL people, regardless of age and colour."

When I leave here, I will leave this earth as a blessed person. I have been blessed with health, wealth, and happiness throughout my life. I have been able to build social capital, to build institutions in my community, my country, and the world. I have lived as a person of great integrity. So I have nothing but praise for life. I have nothing but optimism for the future.

As Mama told me, every day I wake up, I make history. Today is the history that I created yesterday. Most people do not want to say that life has given them what they deserve. I believe that I have gotten what I deserve—the good things and the bad things.

The health, wealth, and happiness we achieve in our lives is directly proportional to the love we invest in the world. Life lived as a labor of love is a sublimely rewarding experience. Please, my brothers and sisters, share your love and taste the joy of life.

Coda: Dreaming and Harvesting

"Dream big dreams, Anthony," Mama taught me, "and work hard to get where you want to go."

I dreamed of being a success, of getting out of Charleston, West Virginia, of earning a college degree, of having a good job, of playing an important role in my community, of being wealthy. When I was younger, all these goals were defined by the Establishment notions of success. As I developed as a human being, they took on a deeper, richer meaning—a meaning defined by the values Mama had taught me as a child.

As I came to understand reality, knowledge, humanity, wisdom, truth, patience, and love, I learned to think of success in terms of health, wealth, and happiness. And I learned how to empower myself and set myself free from the bonds of conventional Establishment wisdom by not giving the ruling cabal power over my mood.

Ironically, the more self-empowered I became, the more independent in my thought, the more I found myself back with Mama, in the close-knit Black community of my childhood. The years of self-discovery had brought me to the man molded by Mama, Billie,

Mrs. Norman, Dr. Fitzhugh, Mr. Barnes, Mr. Calloway, and scores and scores of other people who poured their love into me.

Today, I consider myself a success because I know that these people would be proud of the person I have become. Mama would be pleased to see that I have lived my life according to the values she taught me. She would be pleased to see a person who has not succumbed to hatred of other people, who has not succumbed to self-hatred, who has not succumbed to being a victim because the world is not fair, and who certainly is a person who accepts a supreme power.

And when frustration overtakes me because my dreams are misunderstood or not shared, Mama is the force that keeps me moving forward. She cannot leave me because she is a part of me. That is the beauty of having a mama like I had: She is always with me, because she is who I am.

Mama taught me to dream big dreams, and the dream I am dreaming is of an Aframerican community that has broken the bonds of physical and psychological dependence and has empowered itself with economic and political freedom.

As I said before, Mama taught me that nothing succeeds like success. That is the foundation of my self-empowerment philosophy, and I have been bringing Mama's message to the Aframerican community for over three decades as the host and producer of *Tony Brown's Journal,* as an educator, as a radio show host, as a writer, as an empowerment activist, and as a human being, the role of which I am most proud.

After finding my way back to Mama in this book, I have been able to distill the wisdom from the past and choose the seeds for the future. As a result, I am more committed than ever to serving the causes of equality and self-empowerment through my work.

I will continue to fight the fear with the aphorism of Kent M. Keith: "If you are successful you win false friends and true enemies. Succeed anyway." As a nineteen-year-old student at Harvard, Keith (not Mother Teresa, to whom these aphorisms are widely attributed) also advised: "The good you do will be forgotten tomorrow. Do good anyway."

Among those who believe they have connected to something greater than themselves, this phenomenon is called the Work. Mama was "called" and she trained me for my "calling." As the *Star Wars* movies assert, there is no escaping your fate—and why would you want to?

The (good) Work is simply learning to love others as you love yourself—the way Mama loved me, the son who did not come from her womb. Mama did not invent love and truth, she just captured it from the universal energies available to all of us—not for herself but for the world family.

Because she believed in a carpenter, this maid and dishwasher, to whom I owe my life, has sent this book to you—with all of her love—to make you stronger and your life better. Mama is the Work, the life energy, that came into my life and, I hope, into yours.

I will continue my work, because I want all of my brothers and sisters from every cultural ancestry to say at the end of the day, "I am a success because I have become a person Mama would be proud of." That is health, wealth, and happiness.

Now that you have read this book, Mama is in you, her spirit is there to light your way. Teach tolerance with your actions. Go forth and create the life you want for yourself, your children, and the whole human family.

Acknowledgments

Because writing a book is such a laborious and complex undertaking, authors usually adopt the practice of acknowledging the people who have assisted in the development of the project. I am following that tradition. This book is a departure from my first two books. While it captures my ideas, as did *Black Lies, White Lies: The Truth According to Tony Brown* and *Empower the People,* this book, *What Mama Taught Me,* also captures my heart. Ironically, I had not intended for that to ever happen.

Why should I? I don't have the latest sales figures on *Empower,* but *Black Lies, White Lies* has sold over 100,000 copies. If it ain't broke, don't fix it, I figured. Besides, people can be mean. Despite my best efforts, however, the book that I chased wouldn't come out of its hiding place. The entire world seemed to be conspiring against its birth.

A confluence of events, precipitated mainly by the editor of *Mama,* Henry Ferris, turned history in another direction. The result is what you have read between these covers. The direction in which I would have taken the reader without his editorial direction would have been dramatically different—and, in reflection, a grave mistake and, most of all, a lost opportunity.

Had I succeeded, Carla Fine and Alexander Kopelman, freelance editors, and Karen Smith—the three people to whom I am most indebted—would never have met Mama and I would not have completed my journey back home. For helping me to get there, I thank Carla for applying her enormous literary background and experience in writing seven books to structure the development process. Carla also turned out to be a true friend.

Karen, my administrative assistant, in-house production manager, and best friend, did what she has done on my previous two books. She nursed every word from its inception to the final manuscript and provided invaluable nuances, probably unknown to herself, that led me to many editorial discoveries.

Alex, more than anyone else, helped me to realize Mama. Probably because she became his mama, too. As I talked about my experiences with Mama and explained her philosophy of life, it became clear that Alex is as intuitive as he is brilliant. I was impressed by his ability to extrapolate the core issues and organize them into chapters. We would write and edit back and forth until on one occasion, while finishing Chapter 6, we simultaneously (via e-mail) shared the fact that both of us had cried before reaching page 6.

"Mama's voice is definitely captured in this book," I wrote. Alex responded, "I am so glad I have gotten to meet Mama, through you." We both speculated as to why Mama waited until Chapter 6 to let us know that she was writing the book. Every writer searches for his or her "voice." In this instance, the "voice" belongs to Mama.

All in all, Alex helped me chip away the layers of defense that had covered up the awesome memories of Mama. I don't think that she would have talked to just anyone. I acknowledge that Alex must be a pretty special guy for Mama to have adopted him also.

I needed to go beyond the normal point of departure to write this book—and I needed a medium, someone to reconnect me to deeply buried and sometimes painful feelings. I had previously vowed to myself never to tell anyone who I really was, to take to the grave my private life. I was motivated by the belief that most people are just too damn nosy, and too many others, with empty lives, want personal information about others to practice their voodoo brand of pseudo–pop psychology.

In our sessions, Alex helped me see how my pain could help relieve the pain of many others and how Mama's love, which only I felt, was too valuable to be enjoyed by just one person. Mama, I came to realize, was a national treasure who needed to be shared, notwithstanding the personal risk I would have to take.

Carla, Karen, and Alex helped me see the need to take that risk. I am a better person for it, and I have been blessed with these friends who have helped me introduce you to a maid and dishwasher who worshiped a carpenter. Mama would have taken every needy child in the world under her wing, were it possible. I was just the lucky one.

I acknowledge my friends for helping me find my way back home.

Notes

Introduction

1. *Vanity Fair*, March 2001, p. 277.
2. USA Snapshots, *USA Today,* July 7, 2002, p. D1.
3. Jay Tolson, "Who-am I2,"*U.S. News & World Report,* June 12, 2000, p. 50.

2. Knowledge

1. Matthew 25:14–30.

3. Humanity

1. Marc Lacey, "Fighting 'Light Skin' as a Standard of Beauty," *New York Times,* June 15, 2002, International Section, p. A4.
2. Anthony Summers, *Official and Confidential: The Secret Life of J. Edgar Hoover* (New York: Putnam, 1993), pp. 349–350.
3. Ibid.
4. Linda Villarosa, "Beyond Black and White," *New York Times,* January 1, 2002, Science Times, p. F5.

5. Darryl Fears, "Mixed-Race Heritage, Mixed Emotions," *Washington Post,* April 16, 2001, p. 1.

6. Villarosa, "Beyond Black and White," p. F5.

7. John Seabrook, "The Tree of Me," *New Yorker,* March 26, 2001, p. 58.

8. Ibid., p. 66

9. Josh Fischman, "A Fresh Start," *U.S. News & World Report,* July 22, 2002, p. 38.

10. Ibid.

11. John Noble Wilford, "Redrawing Humanity's Family Tree," *New York Times,* August 6, 2002, Science Times, p. F1.

12. Fischman, "A Fresh Start," p. 38.

13. Nancy Shute, "Tracing Your Genetic Roots: DNA Mapping Is Unraveling the Mystery of Human Origins," *U.S. News & World Report,* January 29, 2001, cover story.

14. Nancy Shute, "Where We Come From," *U.S. News & World Report,* January 29, 2001, p. 34

15. Ibid., p. 36.

16. Mark Hyman, *Blacks Before America III* (Trenton, N.J.: Africa World Press, 1999), p. 14

17. Ibid.

18. Steve Olson, "The Royal We," *Atlantic,* May 2002, p. 62.

19. Tunku Varadarajan, "All About Eve, Our African Mother," *The Wall Street Journal,* April 19, 2002, p. W7.

20. Michael Starr, "It's the Mother of All Scientific Theories," *New York Post,* April 17, 2002, p. 85.

21. Varadarajan, "All About Eve," p. W7.

22. Ibid.

23. Chris Rock, "Notebook Verbatim," *Time,* June 17, 2002, p. 17.

24. Betsy Hart, "A Good Spanking," *New York Post,* June 20, 2002, p. 23.

25. Ibid.

26. Ibid.

27. Ibid.

28. Jeffrey C. Stewart, *1001 Things Everyone Should Know About African American History* (New York: Main Street Books, 1996), p. 129.

4. Wisdom

1. Randy Krehbiel, "Opportunity Lies in Adversity, Speaker Says," *Tulsa World,* June 3, 2002, p. 1.
2. "How to Be a Muslim in America," *Tony Brown's Journal,* no. 2427, November 9, 2001.
3. Andrew Borowiec, "Europeans Wary of Political Islam," *The Washington Times,* September 22, 2002, p. A08.
4. Ibid.
5. David E. Kaplan, "Made in the U.S.A.: Hundreds of Americans Have Followed the Path to Jihad; Here's How and Why," *U.S. News & World Report,* June 10, 2002, p. 18.
6. Gregory Lewis, "Jokes Cut Too Close for Some," *South Florida Sun-Sentinel,* October 2, 2002, p. 22A.
7. Steve Olson, "The Royal We," *Atlantic,* May 2002, p. 62.
8. Tony Brown, *Black Lies, White Lies: The Truth According to Tony Brown* (New York: William Morrow, 1995), pp. 235–236.
9. Ibid., p. 236.
10. Jeffrey C. Stewart, *1001 Things Everyone Should Know About African American History* (New York: Main Street Books, 1996), p. 129.
11. "Thirty Years After Kerner Report, Some Say Racial Divide Wider," CNN.com, March 1, 1998.

5. Truth

1. Catriona Bonthron Gannon and Jamin K. Williams, "Unsung Heroes," *New York Post,* February 13, 2002.
2. Michael H. Cottman, "Do Unto Yourself: *Tony Brown's Journal* Preaches Self-Determination," *New York Newsday*, February 19, 1989, p. 81.
3. *60 Minutes,* April 4, 1999.
4. Ibid.
5. "For BET, Some Static in the Picture," Paul Farhi, *Washington Post,* November 22, 1999, p. C01.

6. Prospectus, BET Holdings, Inc. filed with the Securities and Exchange Commission, October 28, 1991, p. 6.

7. *60 Minutes.*

8. Paul Farhi, "For BET, Some Static in the Picture," p. C01.

9. *60 Minutes.*

10. Cora Daniels, "The 50 Most Powerful Black Executives in America," *Fortune,* July 22, 2002, p. 70.

11. Ibid., p. 72.

6. Patience

1. Isabel Wilkerson, "The Most Powerful Woman in the World," *Essence,* February 2002, p. 118.

2. Richard Poe, *The Wave 4 Way to Building Your Downline* (Roseville, Calif.: Prima Publishing, 2000), p. 106.

3. Jim Hopkins, "Asian Business Owners Gaining Clout," *USA Today,* February 27, 2002, p. 1A.

4. Cliff Hocker and Sakina P. Spruell, "Bad Hair Days," *Black Enterprise,* November 2000, p. 148.

5. Hopkins, "Asian Business Owners Gaining Clout," p. 1A.

6. Ibid.

7. Louis Uchitelle, "Stagnant Wages Pose Added Risks to Weak Economy," *New York Times,* August 11, 2002, p. A1.

8. Steve Lopez, "The Immigration Bomb," *Los Angeles Times,* July 26, 2002, Metro Section, p. 1.

9. Janny Scott, "Immigration Cut into Income in New York, Census Finds," *New York Times,* August 6, 2002, p. A1.

10. Editorial, "The AP's Analyst," *New York Post,* August 7, 2002, p. 26.

11. Janny Scott, "Immigration Cut into Income in New York, Census Finds," p. A1.

12. Ibid.

13. Roy H. Beck, *The Case Against Immigration* (New York: W. W. Norton, 1996).

14. Janny Scott, "Immigration Cut into Income in New York, Census Finds," p. A1.

15. Ibid.

16. www.npg.org/Roper.

17. Thomas D. Elias, "Mexico: Out-flow Won't Stop," *San Francisco Examiner,* July 9, 2002, p. 17A.

18. Donald Lyons, "Upbeat, Uplifting Uptown Tribute," *New York Post,* August 7, 2002, p. 68.

19. Thomas A. Fogarty, "Homeowners Appreciate Rising Values," *USA Today,* February 26, 2002, p. B1.

20. Ibid.

21. Ibid.

22. Ibid.

23. Ibid.

24. *USA* Snapshots, "Career Changes Ahead," *USA Today,* July 29, 2001, p. 1.

25. Mike Lupica, "Grandest Tiger Hears New York's Roar," New York *Daily News,* June 17, 2002, p. 2.

26. Jill Lieber, "Tiger: Major Domination," *USA Today,* June 17, 2002, p. C1.

27. Cora Daniels, "The 50 Most Powerful Black Executives in America," *Fortune,* July 22, 2002, p. 60.

28. Carmen Brown, "Oscar Drought for African-Americans Finally Ends," *Caribbean Life,* March 26, 2002, p. 32.

29. Brian Lewis, "Hoosiers Go Forth," *New York Post,* March 24, 2002, p. 100.

30. Bob Herbert, "An Unlikely Coach," *New York Times,* January 24, 2002, p. A27.

31. Laurence McQuillan, "Bush Dominates Most Admired Poll," *USA Today,* December 27, 2001, p. A3.

32. Ellis Cose, "The New Color of Power," *Newsweek,* January 28, 2002, p. 42.

33. Johnnie L. Roberts, "The Three Who Rose to the Top," *Newsweek,* January 28, 2002, p. 46.

34. Associated Press, February 15, 2002.

35. Wilkerson, "Most Powerful Woman," p. 118.

36. Lynnette Clemetson, "A Young Congressman Looks Back—And Forward," *Newsweek,* January 28, 2002, p. 51.

7. Love

1. Luke 15:11–32.

INDEX